SEEKING PROTECTION:
Addressing Sexual and Domestic Violence in Tanzania's Refugee Camps

Human Rights Watch Women's Rights Division

GW00546089

Human Rights Watch
New York · Washington · London · Brussels

ISBN:1-56432-247-5
Library of Congress Card number: 12017842

Cover photo by Women's Commission for Refugee Women and Children
Cover design by Rafael Jiménez

Addresses for Human Rights Watch
350 Fifth Avenue, 34th Floor, New York, NY 10118-3299
Tel: (212) 290-4700, Fax: (212) 736-1300, E-mail: hrwnyc@hrw.org

1630 Connecticut Avenue, N.W., Suite 500, Washington, DC 20009
Tel: (202) 612-4321, Fax: (202) 612-4333, E-mail: hrwdc@hrw.org

33 Islington High Street, N1 9LH London, UK
Tel: (171) 713-1995, Fax: (171) 713-1800, E-mail: hrwatchuk@gn.apc.org

15 Rue Van Campenhout, 1000 Brussels, Belgium
Tel: (2) 732-2009, Fax: (2) 732-0471, E-mail:hrwatcheu@skynet.be

Web Site Address: http://www.hrw.org

Listserv address: To subscribe to the list, send an e-mail message to
majordomo@igc.apc.org with "subscribe hrw-news" in the body of the message
(leave the subject line blank).

Human Rights Watch is dedicated to
protecting the human rights of people around the world.

We stand with victims and activists to prevent
discrimination, to uphold political freedom, to protect people from inhumane
conduct in wartime, and to bring offenders to justice.

We investigate and expose
human rights violations and hold abusers accountable.

We challenge governments and those who hold power to end abusive practices
and respect international human rights law.

We enlist the public and the international
community to support the cause of human rights for all.

HUMAN RIGHTS WATCH

Human Rights Watch conducts regular, systematic investigations of human rights abuses in some seventy countries around the world. Our reputation for timely, reliable disclosures has made us an essential source of information for those concerned with human rights. We address the human rights practices of governments of all political stripes, of all geopolitical alignments, and of all ethnic and religious persuasions. Human Rights Watch defends freedom of thought and expression, due process and equal protection of the law, and a vigorous civil society; we document and denounce murders, disappearances, torture, arbitrary imprisonment, discrimination, and other abuses of internationally recognized human rights. Our goal is to hold governments accountable if they transgress the rights of their people.

Human Rights Watch began in 1978 with the founding of its Europe and Central Asia division (then known as Helsinki Watch). Today, it also includes divisions covering Africa, the Americas, Asia, and the Middle East. In addition, it includes three thematic divisions on arms, children's rights, and women's rights. It maintains offices in New York, Washington, Los Angeles, London, Brussels, Moscow, Dushanbe, and Bangkok. Human Rights Watch is an independent, nongovernmental organization, supported by contributions from private individuals and foundations worldwide. It accepts no government funds, directly or indirectly.

The staff includes Kenneth Roth, executive director; Michele Alexander, development director; Reed Brody, advocacy director; Carroll Bogert, communications director; Barbara Guglielmo, finance director; Jeri Laber special advisor; Lotte Leicht, Brussels office director; Patrick Minges, publications director; Susan Osnos, then-associate director; Maria Pignataro Nielsen, human resources director; Jemera Rone, counsel; Malcolm Smart, program director; Wilder Tayler, legal and policy director; and Joanna Weschler, United Nations representative. Jonathan Fanton is the chair of the board. Robert L. Bernstein is the founding chair.

The regional directors of Human Rights Watch are Peter Takirambudde, Africa; José Miguel Vivanco, Americas; Sidney Jones, Asia; Holly Cartner, Europe and Central Asia; and Hanny Megally, Middle East and North Africa. The thematic division directors are Joost R. Hiltermann, arms; Lois Whitman, children's; and Regan Ralph, women's.

The members of the board of directors are Jonathan Fanton, chair; Lisa Anderson, Robert L. Bernstein, David M. Brown, William Carmichael, Dorothy Cullman, Gina Despres, Irene Diamond, Adrian W. DeWind, Fiona Druckenmiller, Edith Everett, Michael E. Gellert, Vartan Gregorian, Alice H. Henkin, James F. Hoge, Stephen L. Kass, Marina Pinto Kaufman, Bruce Klatsky, Joanne Leedom-Ackerman, Josh Mailman, Yolanda T. Moses, Samuel K. Murumba, Andrew Nathan, Jane Olson, Peter Osnos, Kathleen Peratis, Bruce Rabb, Sigrid Rausing, Orville Schell, Sid Sheinberg, Gary G. Sick, Malcolm Smith, Domna Stanton, John J. Studzinski, and Maya Wiley. Robert L. Bernstein is the founding chair of Human Rights Watch.

ACKNOWLEDGMENTS

This report is based on research conducted in Tanzania in May and June 1998 and October and November 1999 by Rumbi Mabuwa, researcher with the Women's Rights Division; Binaifer Nowrojee, senior researcher with the Africa division; and LaShawn Jefferson, deputy director of the women's rights division. Rumbi Mabuwa wrote the report with contributions from Binaifer Nowrojee and LaShawn Jefferson. It was edited by LaShawn Jefferson, deputy director of the women's rights division; Regan Ralph, executive director of the women's rights division; Cynthia Brown, then program director of Human Rights Watch; Malcolm Smart, program director of Human Rights Watch; and Dinah PoKempner, general counsel of Human Rights Watch. Specialized readers included Rachael Reilly, refugee policy director of Human Rights Watch; Binaifer Nowrojee; and Alison DesForges, consultant to the Africa division. Kerry McArthur, Laura Rusu, and Tejal Jesrani, associates with the Women's Rights Division, provided invaluable production assistance.

Our special thanks go to Mary Diaz, executive director of the Women's Commission for Refugee Women and Children, for her invaluable editorial contributions. Also, the research assistance of intern Sue Robinson, an Australian lawyer, is gratefully acknowledged.

Human Rights Watch thanks UNHCR and its staff in Geneva and Tanzania for their assistance in arranging our November 1999 mission to Tanzania. We also owe a special debt of gratitude to the NGOs that helped us logistically in Tanzania. We are grateful to the groups, donor governments, and the Tanzanian government, who helped us craft recommendations to UNHCR at their Executive Committee (EXCOM) Standing Committee meeting in Geneva in February 1999. Our thanks go to the African Office for Development and Cooperation, Care International, Caritas International, the International Council on Voluntary Agencies, the International Federation of the Red Cross and Red Crescent Societies, the Steering Committee for Humanitarian Response, the International Rescue Committee (IRC), the International Save the Children Alliance, the Jesuit Refugee Service, Lutheran World Federation, Médecins Sans Frontières, Oxfam, Pro Femmes-Twese Hamwe (Rwanda) (Women Together as One), the Women's Commission on Refugee Women and Children, the World Council of Churches, and Union Aid for Afghan Refugees.

We would also like to thank our funders, without whose continuous support and generosity we could not do our work. In particular, the Moriah Fund, the Ford Foundation, the Shaler Adams Foundation, the Sandler Family Supporting Fund, and the John D. and Catherine T. MacArthur Foundation should be acknowledged for their commitment to supporting improved protection of women's rights in a refugee context.

Most of all, we would like to thank the Burundian women refugees interviewed for this report, the Tanzanian women's groups, and all of the organizations working with the refugees who gave us their invaluable cooperation.

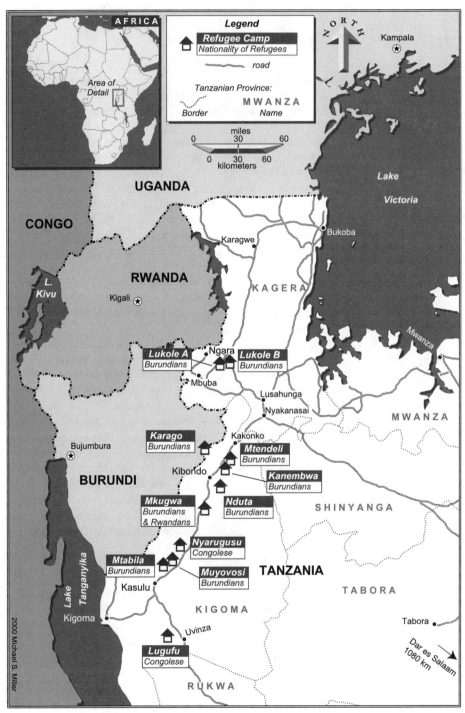

Refugee Camps in Northwest Tanzania

CONTENTS

I. SUMMARY

Women who flee their homes in search of sanctuary from violence too often find that there is no meaningful refuge—they have simply escaped violence in conflict to face a different type of violence in the refugee camps. Women face particular protection and security risks in refugee camps, as well as the challenges of heading households while suffering from their disadvantaged status as women. Refugee women are vulnerable to rape, sexual assault, and other forms of sexual violence. Levels of domestic violence are also high in many refugee communities: in refugee settings, pressures regarding housing, food, security, and other resources often strain domestic situations and erupt in violence. Moreover, extended networks of family, neighbors, and community leaders that may have acted as a deterrent to abuse under normal circumstances no longer exist in the abnormal conditions and unfamiliar territory to which women refugees are exposed. Yet, generally women refugees have limited, or no, legal remedies against sexual and domestic violence, due to their unfamiliarity with, and wariness of, local police and judicial authorities, and because of a lack of proactive, timely, systematic, and sensitive responses by the relevant international and local authorities.

Human Rights Watch began monitoring the situation of Burundian refugees in the Tanzanian camps in 1997. Late that year, we received reports that human rights abuses, particularly sexual violence, were occurring at high rates in the camps, and that the responses of the office of the United Nations High Commissioner for Refugees (UNHCR) and the Tanzanian government to sexual violence were inadequate. Human Rights Watch undertook a first mission to the Tanzanian refugee camps in May and June 1998. Our purposes were to obtain firsthand information about human rights violations, including sexual and other gender-based violence against refugees residing in those camps; and to remind the relevant authorities of their responsibility to ensure that perpetrators of such abuses must be held to account for their actions. We focused on Burundian refugees because they constituted the largest group, approximately two-thirds of the total number who also included refugees from the Democratic Republic of Congo and Rwanda.

In both 1998 and 1999, Human Rights Watch and other rights groups found that Burundian women refugees in the Tanzanian camps were subject to high levels of sexual and domestic violence and urged UNHCR to adopt and implement policies and procedures that would afford refugee women greater protection from, and effective remedies against, these abuses. Many of the refugee women interviewed by Human Rights Watch bore scars and other physical evidence of beatings by their husbands or partners. Some had received such severe injuries that they had required hospital treatment. In addition, it was evident that Burundian women refugees were vulnerable to rape both by male refugees and local Tanzanian nationals. We learned that women were liable to be attacked while carrying out routine, daily tasks, such as gathering firewood, collecting vegetables, or searching for employment in local Tanzanian villages.

But the full extent of the violence was impossible to gauge. Statistics on rape and domestic violence in the Tanzanian refugee camps are unreliable: no comprehensive reporting mechanisms exist, and many cases are believed never to come to light. However, UNHCR officials and their community services implementing partners[1] are now making efforts to collect data on rates of domestic and sexual violence in the camps. In May 1999, Refugees International, a U.S.-based nongovernmental advocacy group, on the basis of a survey they had carried out, estimated that one in four Burundian refugee women in northern Tanzania had been the victim of rape or serious sexual harassment.[2] The International Rescue Committee (IRC), a US-based humanitarian organization that provides health and other social services to refugees in the Tanzanian camps, including an education and counseling program for women who are victims of gender-based violence, documented 122 cases of rape and 613 cases of domestic violence in four camps—Kanembwa, Mkugwa, Mtendeli, and Nduta, in 1998. In 1999, the figures were 111 cases of rape and 764 cases of domestic violence. Some of the rape cases had been referred to police for investigation. Domestic violence cases, however, were mostly handled outside the justice system, through counseling. The example of Burundian women refugees in Tanzania shows all too clearly how the absence of well-designed and concrete programs to protect women refugees from violence and to punish the perpetrators of such violence when it occurs, leads to high rates of domestic and sexual violence. Their experiences also show why it is imperative that those responsible for the welfare and protection of refugees, notably the host government and UNHCR, recognize and respond effectively to such abuses from the earliest stage of the refugee influx. Humanitarian organizations long complained about the high rates of sexual and domestic violence in the Tanzanian refugee camps and bemoaned the lack of an effective response. Since the establishment of the camps some six years ago, these organizations, some of which are UNHCR's implementing partners, have been working to improve programs and services to women victims of violence. However, prior to 1999, they received little or no assistance from UNHCR.

---

[1] UNHCR enters into contract with humanitarian aid organizations to provide a variety of services to refugees. These are its implementing partners.
[2] Refugees International, *Hope in the Fight to Reduce Gender Violence in Tanzanian Refugee Camps* (Washington, DC: Refugees International, May 26, 1999).

UNHCR's shortcomings in responding to the problem of violence against women in the camps prior to 1999 occurred despite the agency's own longstanding directives on preventing and responding to gender-based violence. UNHCR has issued two important sets of guidelines to provide direction to their staff on ways to better protect women refugees.[3]   However, these guidelines have often represented little more than theory, with few, if any, efforts made by UNHCR staff to ensure that they form a routine and integral part of all UNHCR programs from the very first stage of any refugee crisis. Too often, women refugees have been left languishing in camps with little or no attention paid to their protection needs—even in situations in which UNHCR and the host government are informed of the violence being perpetrated against refugee women.

In 1999, five years after the establishment of the refugee camps in Tanzania, UNHCR began more systematically to address violence against women in these camps by both implementing new programs and strengthening existing ones. These efforts were undertaken partly in response to pressure from human rights groups, including Human Rights Watch, and UNHCR's receipt in October 1998 of funds to support programs to combat violence against refugee women in Tanzania and other African countries. Many of these programs are commendable, but further reforms are needed to ensure that they provide refugee women the greatest possible degree of protection.

As this report goes to publication, UNHCR's programs on violence against women in the Tanzanian camps could be further strengthened in several ways. With regard to domestic violence, first, no protocol exists to guide both UNHCR staff and other refugees who counsel victims of domestic violence, nor has UNHCR yet developed an explicit set of policy guidelines on domestic violence for use by its staff. This absence of a clear, informed, and consistent UNHCR policy on domestic violence is a significant omission, and one that may lead to women's lives being jeopardized. That said, however, Human Rights Watch is pleased to note that UNHCR has now recognized the need to revise its policies on refugee women to include guidelines on domestic violence and urges UNHCR to consult with and involve NGOs, particularly those with expertise in working with refugee women.

A second problem in relation to domestic violence is that there are no applicable mechanisms within the refugee camps to punish perpetrators of domestic violence against women and most of these cases are not referred to local authorities.

---

[3] A synopsis of *Sexual Violence against Refugees: Guidelines on Prevention and Response* can be found on the Women's Commission for Refugee Women and Children website: http://www.intrescom.org/wcrwc/wc_guidelinesexviol.html. For full text of the guidelines, contact UNHCR.

There are no guiding principles or mechanisms to monitor and ensure that mediation councils known in *Kirundi*, the language of Burundi, as *abashingatahe*. These councils are run by mostly male refugee elders and do not preside over criminal cases. Neither UNHCR nor the Tanzanian authorities have communicated to the abashingatahe that their power to mediate disputes does not give them jurisdiction to preside over alleged criminal actions. Among other things, these councils preside over cases of domestic violence, though their standards are not based on relevant international human rights law. UNHCR and the Tanzanian authorities need to communicate clearly to the abashingatahe that any disputes brought to their attention, when involving physical violence occurring in domestic or non-domestic settings, should be referred for criminal investigation. Finally, UNHCR's education and counseling programs on domestic violence lack a core message on women's equality and are not implemented consistently across the various refugee camps. Together, these factors seriously weaken UNHCR's programs to respond to domestic violence, often resulting in refugee women having to suffer domestic violence in the Tanzanian camps with little or no recourse.

In some cases, a lack of coordination among protection officers and community services officers has undermined the effective protection of refugees. UNHCR has placed staff in each camp to provide refugees with community services and protection. The community services officers are responsible for developing community-based programs or income generating projects for refugees. They also run all education programs for refugees on sexual and other gender -based violence and provide counseling for the victims of such violence. In some camps, programs are run by implementing partners' staff in collaboration with UNHCR community services officers. UNHCR protection officers are responsible for all matters relating to refugee protection: they oversee camp security, advise refugees on legal matters when they are victims of crime, follow up cases involving refugees to ensure that they are properly investigated and prosecuted, and work with the host government authorities on matters relating to refugee rights under international refugee law. There is, however, a lack of systematic follow-up in cases of sexual violence in the camps, as well as a lack of coordination between community services officers and protection officers in seeking to ensure that women know and understand their legal rights and other options when they have been subjected to sexual or physical assault. In addition, more coordination is needed between community services officers and protection officers to ensure that women receive appropriate assistance, advice, and support during legal proceedings.

One factor contributing to this is that the UNHCR operation in Tanzania functions under stringent budgetary constraints. This also means that UNHCR has insufficient resources to provide refugees with certain basic necessities, such as fuel for cooking and housing. Women often must travel many miles outside the camps to collect firewood, increasing their vulnerability to rape or other sexual assault. UNHCR and the Tanzanian host government have received inadequate financial and other support from the international donor community while sustaining a very heavy burden of mass refugee influxes. Various crises In Africa have taxed UNHCR's resources, while the international donor community's focus on recent refugee crises in Europe has further limited the resources available for UNHCR and host governments to assist African refugees. Resources, however, are only part of the problem. UNHCR's slow progress in fully implementing its own *Guidelines on the Protection of Refugee Women* (hereafter *Guidelines on Refugee Women*) has also stemmed from lack of interest and prejudice among some UNHCR staff, and a lack of political will to make the protection of refugee women a priority.

The situation for both Burundian refugees and local Tanzanians living close to the border is precarious given the potential spillover of rebel activity and arms flow from the Burundian conflict. Robberies, rapes, and thefts of crops from Tanzanian farms have resulted in a growing anti-refugee sentiment among local Tanzanians, sometimes leading to rape and other violence against refugees. In one particularly serious incident in May 1999, a group of some fifty or more refugee women were alleged to have been raped by a group of Tanzanian men, apparently in reprisal for the death of a local school teacher. More than a hundred Tanzanian men were believed to have taken part in the rapes, though only eleven were subsequently arrested.

Human Rights Watch visited the Tanzanian refugee camps in May 1998 and October 1999. During the first visit, Human Rights Watch researchers interviewed refugee leaders, representatives of UNHCR, the United Nations Children's Fund (UNICEF), and other humanitarian organizations, as well as Tanzanian government officials from the judiciary, the police, and the Ministry of Home Affairs (MHA), which is responsible for refugee matters. Human Rights Watch visited eight refugee camps—Kanembwa, Lukole A and B, Mtabila 1 and 2, Mtendeli, Muyovosi, and Nduta—and interviewed over one hundred refugee women, including twenty-seven who had been victims of domestic or sexual violence while in the refugee camps. Following this first visit, Human Rights Watch visited UNHCR's headquarters in Geneva, Switzerland, in February 1999, to discuss its findings and make recommendations to UNHCR and donor governments. In June 1999, a Human Rights Watch delegation visited Dar-es-Salaam, Tanzania, where UNHCR's Tanzania field office is headquartered, to hold discussions with the Tanzanian authorities and with UNHCR. Finally, a follow-up mission to the camps was carried out in October and November 1999 in order to assess steps being taken to respond to the problem of violence against refugee women.

In 1998, we found that some UNHCR staff were defensive or dismissive about the problem of violence against women refugees. Some even tended to blame the victim, while others saw such violence as unfortunate, but "normal,"or attributed sexual violence to Burundian culture. At that time, UNHCR lacked both community services staff with relevant training, and dedicated programs to assist refugee women.

When Human Rights Watch returned to the camps in 1999, we found that UNHCR, to its considerable credit, had initiated more systematic, careful, and effective efforts to address the problem of sexual violence. Together with its implementing partners, UNHCR had begun to put in place a stronger safety net for women victims of violence by expanding and strengthening its existing programs to combat violence against refugee women. These new programs are aimed at raising community awareness of sexual and other gender-based violence; providing counseling for victims of sexual violence; following up rape cases with the police and courts to ensure that they are investigated and that perpetrators are prosecuted; and establishing food distribution systems to ensure women's access to food, particularly in situations of domestic violence or divorce.

Since March 1999, there has also been increased coordination between UNHCR and its implementing partners, as well as with local NGOs working with refugees, in setting up programs to address violence against women in the camps. UNHCR has also hired new staff specifically to implement programs for refugee women. For example, two Sexual and Gender-Based Violence (SGBV) assistants were recruited in September 1999. Their responsibilities include collaborating with community services officers to implement programs for refugee women and following up on cases that require community-based assistance. Two Tanzanian lawyers were also appointed in September 1999 to assist refugee women who are willing to bring cases of violence against them before the courts, and an international security liaison officer was recruited to train police deployed to refugee camps on their responsibilities in refugee situations and to monitor their work.

Human Rights Watch welcomes UNHCR's efforts to increase protection of refugee women in the Tanzanian camps. Such developments show what can be achieved with political will and the appropriate allocation of resources. While it will clearly take some time for these measures to have their full effect, they appear to be a step in the right direction and, if ultimately successful, they could usefully be adapted and replicated in other UNHCR programs elsewhere.

Three issues, however, remain to be resolved. First, delivery and distribution of food and non-food items to refugees in the camps are not sufficiently responsive to the needs of women victims of domestic violence. Under UNHCR's food distribution system, refugee heads of household receive the food for their families.

When it reaches the household, women are responsible for the cooking, but men retain the power to decide how the food is used. Some sell the family's ration or parts of it, keeping the money they receive for their own personal use. Women refugees complained to Human Rights Watch that, as a result, they and their children were sometimes left without enough to eat and, when they complained about this to their husbands, they were beaten. Second, while it is women who collect firewood for their family fuel allocation and grow crops to supplement their food rations, the areas where they can do this are often distant from the camps and from police protection, increasing women's vulnerability to sexual assault. Last, UNHCR's lack of explicit policy guidelines on responding to domestic violence leaves its staff without direction or training on how to prevent and address the problem. In 1999, Human Rights Watch found that UNHCR had adopted a protocol which lays out clear procedures for staff to follow for reporting rape, but not for domestic violence. Moreover, although UNHCR had instructed the abashingatahe not to deal with cases of rape, no similar restrictions were communicated to the abashingatahe forbidding them from dealing with cases of domestic violence. This left the abashingatahe with the discretion to preside over and mete out punishments in domestic violence cases—frequently passing judgements that did not conform with the requirements of international human rights law.

UNHCR has overall responsibility for camp administration, but the Tanzanian host government also has a responsibility, among other things, to extend police protection and judicial redress to all refugees—including victims of rape and domestic violence—through its domestic legal system. However, the Tanzanian justice system is generally overburdened and underfunded, and it does not adequately investigate, prosecute, and punish perpetrators of sexual and domestic violence. Despite the existence of laws punishing rape and assault, the Tanzanian authorities' lack of resources, guidance, and training to enforce those laws has left women with little hope of seeing their attackers held accountable. Moreover, we found that investigators seldom sought to obtain the evidence required to prosecute a domestic violence case because of a prevailing bias against the state intervening in "private" domestic matters. Tanzanian police officers interviewed by Human Rights Watch did not regard domestic violence as a crime, though they were concerned about sexual violence.

Refugee women are also discouraged by other refugees from taking complaints about sexual or domestic violence to the Tanzanian police or courts. Those who do lodge cases often face recrimination and blame from within the refugee community, including from their families, for reporting on fellow refugees rather than seeking assistance from the abashingatahe. Within the camps, refugees depend heavily on the abashingatahe system in which a group of respected, mostly male refugees appointed by the community acts as an arbiter of disputes. Women refugees who are victims of violence often seek their assistance, although the elders are not supposed to deal with serious criminal matters of such magnitude as murder, arson, or rape. They do deal with cases of domestic violence, however, but do not constitute a satisfactory mechanism because, according to Burundian custom, the role of the abashingatahe is reconciliatory. Moreover, the abashingatahe's discriminatory views about women often result in women's claims being minimized.

To conclude, there are several important lessons that can be drawn from the Tanzania case. First, UNHCR needs to ensure a more institutionalized response if it is to address consistently and effectively the protection needs of refugee women from the start of an emergency. Second, UNHCR guidelines on the protection of refugee women and the prevention of sexual violence must be more speedily and consistently implemented in all refugee situations, and UNHCR staff and those of its partner organizations should be fully apprised of, and trained in, their content. Last, UNHCR must address the protection gap for victims of domestic violence and design and implement concrete policy guidelines for its staff on how to prevent and respond to the problem of domestic violence.

II. RECOMMENDATIONS

In the recommendations that follow we highlight steps that need to be taken and monitored to protect refugee women from domestic and sexual violence. In Tanzania, UNHCR has already taken preliminary steps in this direction. These recommendations are intended to be seen as benchmarks against which the actions of UNHCR and host governments can be monitored to ensure that the human rights of refugee women are protected.

To UNHCR

- Adopt and implement concrete policy guidelines on domestic violence to direct staff on how to respond to cases of domestic violence, and monitor their implementation in all camps. These guidelines on domestic violence should, among other things, (1) include directions to medical and community services staff to screen women to identify victims of domestic violence; (2) call for staff to conduct preventive education programs on domestic violence aimed at all refugees; (3) ensure that victims of domestic violence are provided with full information about procedures for obtaining alternate shelter, food ration cards, legal redress, and protection in the event that they want to leave their husbands or partners; and (4) require staff to refer and follow up on all assault cases with the local police and courts.

- UNHCR should also delete section 3.5 of its UNHCR *Sexual Violence against Refugees: Guidelines on Prevention and Response* (hereafter: *Sexual Violence Guidelines*), which discourages UNHCR staff from intervening in sexual violence cases occurring in the home and provide more constructive direction to staff on how best to intervene in situations of marital rape and other domestic abuse.

- Provide greater guidance and support to state justice systems to help ensure that refugee women victims of domestic and sexual violence have effective recourse to redress.

- Ensure that refugee-run dispute resolution mechanisms (such as the abashingatahe in the Tanzanian camps) are instructed that cases involving acts of violence, whether committed in domestic and non-domestic settings, are beyond their jurisdiction and must be referred to the criminal justice authorities for investigation and prosecution.

- Provide alternative fuel sources for refugees in camps to avoid the risk of women being exposed to sexual violence and attack when they leave the camps to collect firewood.

- Ensure that the Gender Advisor for Refugee Women is empowered to ensure that the concerns of refugee women receive high-level priority within UNHCR. In particular, the Gender Advisor for Refugee Women should be given authority and a remit to require full compliance by UNHCR field and headquarters staff with its policies on protection of refugee women, and to monitor such compliance. A set of universal indicators should be established to monitor programs for consistency with the *Guidelines on Refugee Women* and with the *Sexual Violence Guidelines*.

- Ensure that the existing *Guidelines on Refugee Women* are more consistently and expeditiously implemented in all refugee settings, including through the following ways: (1) provide ongoing training for all relevant UNHCR staff, especially community services and protection officers, prior to their deployment in the field, on appropriate responses to and preventive measures against domestic violence, rape, and other crimes of sexual violence; (2) ensure that all divisions of UNHCR monitor and regularly share information with respect to the protection of refugee women, including field staff and at the headquarters level, the regional bureaus, the Divisions of International Protection Inspection and Evaluation, Technical and Operational Support, and Programme and Technical Support; (3) facilitate greater nongovernmental organization (NGO) involvement in monitoring the protection of refugee women by conducting information sharing and training workshops, at both the headquarters and field levels, with NGO and UNHCR staff on protection of refugee women; and (4) hold UNHCR staff responsible for applying the *Guidelines on Refugee Women* from the onset of any refugee emergency.

- As was done by recruiting an international security liaison officer to coordinate and monitor police officers deployed to the Tanzanian camps, ensure that there is a staff person responsible for coordinating all UNHCR's sexual and other gender-based violence (SGBV) programs in the camps in order to ensure that programs are consistently monitored and implemented. The SGBV coordinator should design a work plan for all staff of UNHCR, NGOs, and implementing partners, to maximize effectiveness and improve coordination, cooperation, and non-duplication of activities.

- Establish food monitoring committees composed of refugees, NGO representatives, and UNHCR staff to monitor food management at household levels in order to better ensure that women and children receive their allocated food supply and to prevent refugee men from selling or otherwise misappropriating ration food given for their families.

- On a periodic and timely basis in each camp, identify women victims of domestic violence who may have problems coming forward on their own and offer them any necessary assistance and protection.

- Carry out a study on the viability of establishing shelter homes in the refugee camps to provide victims of domestic violence with safe shelter when they need to hide from their abusers.

- Train all new staff, including police deployed to refugee camps, on the law and services available for rape and domestic violence victims. Inform all new staff and police about their expected duties, including the duty to protect refugees from sexual and domestic violence.

- Compile and maintain in a timely and consistent manner data on all reported incidents of domestic and sexual violence in the camps, showing the number of victims, their ages, and their gender.

To the Tanzanian Government

To protect women refugees from sexual and domestic violence, the Tanzanian government should:

- Ensure that police investigate incidents of violence against women and are given sufficient guidance and training on steps they must follow in the collection of evidence in rape and domestic violence cases. To achieve this objective, develop and communicate policy guidelines directing the police, prosecutors, and magistrates on ways to investigate, prosecute, and punish rape and domestic violence.

- Discipline officers who neglect, dismiss, or attempt to discourage women victims of violence from pursuing their cases.

- Where possible, provide more refugees with plots of land for small-holder cultivation to supplement their relief food supplies. This will diminish the need for refugees to leave the camps to work, farm, or trade and may ease the growing tensions between refugees and Tanzanians.

To International Donors

To ensure high standards of response to sexual and domestic violence in refugee camps globally, as well as in Tanzania, international donors, including the United States, Canada, Japan, Australia, and the member states of the European Union should:

- Continue to provide earmarked financial and logistical support to UNHCR and host governments to improve programs designed for the protection of refugee women from sexual and domestic violence.

- Actively call on UNHCR to (1) better implement its existing *Guidelines on Refugee Women*; (2) adopt explicit guidelines to direct staff on how to prevent and respond to domestic violence in refugee settings; and (3) give the Gender Advisor for Refugee Women the authority to monitor and ensure compliance with UNHCR's stated policies on protection of refugee women in all UNHCR field offices.

- Provide funding, training, and other support to the Tanzanian government to enable it to adopt policies (including those recommended above) to address better sexual and domestic violence against refugee women. The Tanzanian law enforcement and judicial systems are currently overburdened and underfunded. Greater international support for the judiciary and police is required, including, among other things, for training in refugee and human rights law and for programs on preventing, investigating, and prosecuting violence against women.

- Fund alternative fuel sources for refugees in the Tanzanian camps to avoid the risk of exposing women to sexual attacks when they leave the camps to collect firewood.

- Support studies of the viability of establishing shelter homes in the Tanzanian refugee camps to provide victims of domestic violence with safe shelter when they need to hide from their abusers.

• Provide funding to support the appointment of a coordinator for all UNHCR's sexual and gender-based violence programs in the Tanzanian camps to ensure that these programs are consistently monitored and implemented in all camps.

III. BACKGROUND

The Refugee Crisis

Over 380,000[4] refugees from Burundi reside in nine camps administered by UNHCR in Tanzania, close to the country's border with Burundi. Most are members of the Hutu ethnic group who fled to Tanzania between 1993 and 1996 to escape the civil war which erupted in Burundi following the murder of Melchior Ndadaye, the country's first democratically-elected Hutu president, in December 1993.[5] In Burundi's continuing civil war, both government troops and insurgent Hutu opposition groups have slaughtered unarmed civilians and carried out other egregious human rights violations. When Maj. Pierre Buyoya, a former President of Burundi, seized power from a paralyzed civilian government in a July 1996 coup, he claimed that he was seeking to stop the bloodshed that began three years earlier with the murder of Ndadaye. Since the coup, however, the Burundian army and armed Tutsi political groups have engaged in massive violations of human rights against the civilian Hutu population. The coup also triggered country-wide violence in which insurgent Hutu opposition groups have attacked Tutsis.

Tens of thousands of civilians were killed in the conflict sparked by President Ndadaye's murder, and hundreds of thousands fled to Tanzania or other neighboring countries. The massive influx of refugees in the past six years from Rwanda, Burundi, and the Democratic Republic of the Congo has generated anti-refugee sentiment among Tanzanians: increasingly, refugees are viewed by many Tanzanians as a threat to security and a drain on the country's limited resources.[6] At the time this report goes to press, however, Burundian refugees continue to stream into Tanzania. Armed attacks by the Burundian army and rebel forces have intensified since the last quarter of 1999, resulting in the destruction of homes and property and massive forced displacement of civilians. According to Refugees International, a U.S.-based nongovernmental advocacy group, over 21,000 Burundian refugees arrived in Tanzania during December 1999.[7] The outflow of Burundian refugees has continued through the first quarter of 2000 at the rate of

---

[4] UNHCR figures as of September 1999.

[5] For a more in-depth analysis of the civil war, *see* Human Rights Watch, *Proxy Targets: Civilians in War in Burundi* (New York: Human Rights Watch, March 1998).

[6] For a detailed analysis of Tanzania's policy shift toward refugees, *see* Human Rights Watch, "In the Name of Security: Forced Round-Ups of Refugees in Tanzania," *A Human Rights Watch Report*, vol. 11, no. 4, July 1999.

[7] Refugees International, *Tanzanian Camps Now Strained Beyond Capacity* (Washington, DC: Refugees International, January 21, 2000).

approximately 5,000 refugees per week.[8] This influx of refugees is further straining Tanzanian government resources. There are ongoing diplomatic initiatives, led since October 1999 by former South African President Nelson Mandela, who took over chairing the Burundi peace talks from the late former President of Tanzania, Julius Nyerere,[9] to negotiate an end to the war and to restore a multi-party democracy, but these have had little effect as yet in stopping the war.

The Refugee Camps

Most of the ethnic Hutu Burundian refugees in Tanzania live in nine refugee camps overseen by UNHCR in the Ngara and Kigoma sub-regions of western Tanzania: Lukole A and B, in the Ngara area, which accommodate approximately 90,000 refugees; Mtendeli, Kanembwa, Karago, and Nduta, in the Kibondo area of the Kigoma sub-region, where there are approximately 170,000 refugees; and Muyovosi and Mtabila in the Kasulu area, which accommodate a further 90,000 Burundians.[10] In December 1999, the Tanzanian government established Karago camp in response to an increase in the influx of Burundian refugees in the last quarter of 1999.[11] As of January 2000, the Karago camp housed approximately 30,000 Burundian refugees.[12]

Camps in the Kigoma sub-region are located near the towns of Kigoma, Kasulu, and Kibondo, which lie in a remote and underdeveloped area close to Tanzania's border with Burundi. It is difficult to travel between these camps as roads are barely passable, and there are few social amenities, no infrastructure, and no basic services in the Kigoma and Ngara regions—presenting an environment that is extremely difficult for humanitarian aid workers and refugees alike to endure. While conditions in the camps are poor, the camps are considered by UNHCR to be at a "care and maintenance" rather than at an "emergency" stage because all basic services are operational.[13]

---

[8] Ibid.

[9] Former President Julias Nyerere died in October 13, 1999.

[10] UNHCR figures as of February 2000.

[11] Human Rights Watch interview, Judith Mtawali, Director of Refugees, MHA, Tanzania, November 16, 1999. Also *see* Refugees International, *Tanzanian Camps Now Strained Beyond Capacity* (Washington, DC, Refugees International, January 21, 2000).

[12] UNHCR figures as of January 2000.

[13] The term "care and maintenance" is used by UNHCR to refer to camps that have passed from the emergency phase of UNHCR operations to one of normal camp management.

As of November 1999, there were approximately eight local and international NGOs working with refugees in the Tanzanian camps. Among the international NGOs were the IRC, Dutch Relief Agency, Norwegian People's Aid, Christian Outreach, Care International, and Caritas International. These NGOs are all UNHCR implementing partners, and they provide health or other social and community services to refugees. Among the local NGOs working with refugees in the camps were the Diocese of Western Tanganyika and UMATI, an organization that conducts research on health issues and provides health services to refugees. Each organization is responsible for providing specific services in a designated camp. Each camp has a UNHCR protection officer, who is responsible for overseeing all security and protection duties including assisting refugees who are victims of crime with legal advice on how to pursue their cases in court[14] and a UNHCR community services officer who is responsible for designing and running community services programs, such as education, income generation projects, and counseling services for refugees.[15] The community services officers are supposed to work in collaboration with staff of UNHCR's implementing partners in running programs for refugees. There is also a field officer for each camp who, among other things, oversees the camp management, allocates newly arrived refugees with places to live, and distributes plastic sheeting, food, and other supplies.[16]

The Tanzanian government has also placed its own representatives in the camps. These include police, magistrate, and camp commanders. The camp commanders are representatives of MHA and are responsible for overseeing the administration and enforcement of Tanzanian law and policies in the camps.[17] Human Rights Watch, however, found little clarity among Tanzanian authorities and UNHCR staff concerning who bears responsibility for responding to sexual and other gender-based violence. Neither police, magistrates, nor camp commanders held routine meetings with UNHCR officers to discuss and establish a clear procedure

---

[14] Human Rights Watch interview, UNHCR protection officers, Kasulu, Kibondo, and Ngara, Tanzania, October and November 1999.

[15] Human Rights Watch interview, UNHCR community services officers, Kasulu, Kibondo, and Ngara, Tanzania, October and November 1999.

[16] Human Rights Watch interview, UNHCR field officers, Kasulu, Kibondo, and Ngara, Tanzania, October and November 1999.

[17] Human Rights Watch interview, camp commanders, Kasulu, Kibondo, and Ngara, October and November 1999.

for referring cases of domestic violence reported to them.[18] As a result, often cases were circulated from person to person with little effect and leaving the victim confused or discouraged from further reporting or pursuing their cases in court.[19]

To improve camp management and administration, UNHCR and MHA camp commanders have organized the camps into blocks, streets, and plots. In each camp, there are block and street leaders, who are appointed by members of their block on a yearly basis, with UNHCR and MHA camp commanders assisting in organizing the elections. Refugees are also organized into security committees, or *sungu-sungus*, comprised mostly of young men and a few women recruited by UNHCR to patrol the camps.[20] The block and street leaders as well as the sungu-sungus are the key interlocutors between refugees and camp officials. The block and street leaders, together with a network of community elders recognized as abashingatahe,[21] are sources of consultation on various problems among refugees in the camps, including domestic violence disputes. Very few women are elected to positions of leadership however, as block or street leaders, or abashingatahe.[22] To address this problem, UNHCR and humanitarian organizations involved in working with refugees in the camps are organizing committees of refugee women's representatives to involve women in programs and positions of leadership in the camps.

---

[18] Human Rights Watch interviews, camp commander, Kasulu, Tanzania, October 23, 1999; protection officer, Kibondo, Tanzania, November 8, 1999; and police officers, Kibondo, Tanzania, November 6, 1999.

[19] Human Rights Watch interviews, refugee women representatives, Mtabila 1 and 2, Kanembwa, Mtendeli, and Nduta camps; refugee crisis intervention team, Lukole A and B camps, Tanzania, October and November 1999.

[20] Sungu-sungus are provided an incentive of 10,500 Tanzanian shillings (U.S.$13.00) a month. In November 1999 the exchange rate was 800 Tanzanian shillings to one U.S. dollar.

[21] In Burundi, abashingatahe are Burundian men who have gained community respect and recognition as leaders. In Burundi, they serve the community by mediating disputes arising among neighbors, family, and other relations. Basically, this institution is entirely male, with the only exception to include female refugees created as a result of pressure from UNHCR. In the Tanzanian refugee camps, the abashingatahe are Burundian male refugees, with a few women, who preside over cases and disputes arising in the camps. The section below on "Responses by UNHCR" has more information on the function and powers of the abashingatahe in a refugee context.

[22] Human Rights Watch interview, women representatives, Kasulu and Kibondo camps, Tanzania, October and November 1999.

Women's Unequal Status in Burundian Society

As was made clear in Human Rights Watch interviews with Burundian community leaders, including women leaders, as well as UNHCR officials and others, women are traditionally accorded inferior status to men in Burundi. This is also reflected in the camps, exacerbating women's vulnerability to sexual and domestic violence. In Burundian society, women are traditionally considered to be dependents of their male relatives and subordinate to men, who are seen as the natural heads of their households. Most women interviewed by Human Rights Watch received little or no education, had never been employed outside the home, and were totally dependent on their husbands for economic and other support. Most decisions within the family are taken by men, including how the family's resources are to be used, whether children are to attend school, whether and when their wives can leave the home, and when marital sex is to occur. One Burundian refugee woman summed up the situation to Human Rights Watch: "A wife is just like a child in Burundi. She is not supposed to question her husband's decisions."[23]

Responsibilities within the family are also divided firmly according to gender roles. Thus, women are exclusively responsible for child care, obtaining and preparing the family's food, and upkeep of the home. Men, on the other hand, are responsible for building the home, providing the family's income, and deciding how that income is used.

The inferior status of women in Burundian society means that it is generally accepted that they may be physically punished by their husbands when they are considered to have done wrong and that they have no means of redress against such punishment. Some Burundian women and men criticized this in their discussions with Human Rights Watch—but many others sought to justify it as an aspect of Burundian "culture." Men tended to see this violence as the husband's right as head of the household to provide guidance for the family.

Most of the refugee women interviewed by Human Rights Watch had originated from rural areas of Burundi, a largely agricultural society. They said that, even when subjected to severe domestic violence, women almost never complained to the police but, instead, sought redress through the abashingatahe, who could tell their husbands to stop beating them and to give them money or cloth as compensation. In addition, when they were in Burundi, women said that they had first sought assistance from other members of their family, or from friends, neighbors, religious leaders, or community elders, when they had been faced with

---

[23] Human Rights Interview, refugee woman representative, Mtabila 1 camp, Tanzania, November 2, 1999.

domestic violence.[24] Involving the police or judicial authorities, they said, would be done only as a very last resort and, anyway, was often not a practical option due to distance from the nearest police station and the difficulties of travel.[25] Also, seeking the intervention of such official judicial structures would be perceived as bringing shame upon the family and cause a woman to be ostracized, exposing her to the possibility of further violence by her husband. Women told Human Rights Watch that they generally sought to avoid situations that could result in domestic violence, staying at home when their husbands were home, always asking permission when they wished to go somewhere, preparing meals on time, and consenting to sex when their husbands demanded.

Not surprisingly, many of these same attitudes and practices of subordination are also prevalent in the Burundian refugee camps in Tanzania. Here too, women are exclusively responsible for collecting firewood, maintaining the home, and providing child care. Many men, likewise, continue to consider women as their subordinates and show no sign of wishing for or seeing a need to change.

This type of social and economic context is one in which sexual and domestic violence tends to flourish, exacerbated by the particular stresses to which both men and women are exposed in becoming refugees and being required to live in special camps. Despite the efforts of UNHCR, the Tanzanian authorities, and humanitarian organizations, refugees in the camps in Tanzania are subjected to conditions of deprivation, shortages of material resources, cramped conditions, enforced idleness, and poverty leading to drunkenness and other social dysfunction, including high levels of violence against women.

---

[24] Ibid.

[25] Human Rights Watch interviews, refugee women representatives, Mtabila 1 and 2, Kanembwa, Mtendeli, and Nduta camps; and refugee crisis intervention team, Lukole A and B camps, Tanzania, October and November 1999. Also *see* section on "Responses by UNHCR" for details on the mediation and counseling roles of community leaders in Burundi as adapted to the refugee camps and in Burundi.

IV. DOMESTIC VIOLENCE

Scope of the Problem

Domestic violence is a leading cause of female injuries around the world. Women are often targets of domestic violence because of their unequal status in society.[26] Domestic violence usually involves the infliction of bodily injury, accompanied by verbal threats and harassment, emotional and psychological abuse, or the destruction of property, and it is employed usually as a means of coercion, control, revenge, or punishment of a person with whom the abuser is or has been involved in an intimate relationship. The assailant, in fact, frequently blames his violence on the victim and on her behavior and may use the violence to assert his control. As a result, the woman victim may become isolated, cut off from family or community support, and afraid to venture from her home. She may also be made to feel that her inability to avoid abuse at the hands of her intimate partner means that she is somehow inadequate, a failure, even deserving of abuse or powerless to escape it.[27]

Addressing the problem of domestic violence is complex. Many women feel obliged to conceal the fact of their own abuse and to continue to live in violent relationships, because, for example, by being a married woman or having a male partner, they are perceived to have a higher status in their society; or for the sake of their children; due to religious convictions; or by reason of other emotional attachments.

While this report will not present a solution to all of the complexities surrounding the issue of domestic violence, it seeks to identify important forms of recourse and intervention strategies that UNHCR and host governments should adopt when responding to domestic violence in refugee camps. Protecting the rights and responding to the needs of domestic violence victims requires a multi-pronged approach. First, all domestic violence victims are entitled to report abuse to the authorities and to have those authorities conduct a vigorous investigation and

---

[26] Cases of female-perpetrated domestic violence occur in different settings, including in the refugee setting, but more rarely compared to male-perpetrated domestic violence. For example, in group interviews with Burundian refugees in the Tanzanian camps, some male refugees generally complained to Human Rights Watch that they were being beaten by their wives or girlfriends. We did not, however, collect any testimonies of female-perpetrated domestic violence in the camps.

[27] See "Domestic Violence," in Human Rights Watch, *The Human Rights Watch Global Report on Women's Human Rights*, (New York: Human Rights Watch, August 1995) pp.341-409.

prosecution of their complaints. At the same time, women abused by a spouse or intimate partner confront unique difficulties in bringing their attackers to justice and seeking safety for themselves and other family members. They may, for example, be financially dependent on their abuser, reluctant to have their partners jailed or their families break up, or fearful of condemnation by their families or communities should they pursue criminal charges. These and other factors often make women reluctant to bring charges in domestic violence cases or lead them to drop charges already filed. It is critical, therefore, to provide domestic violence victims with complimentary measures of support, such as mediation and counseling by community elders, family or friends. In many cases, women may look to non-litigation community-based mediation and counseling to resolve domestic violence disputes. However, although mediation and counseling may work well in some cases, in others such alternatives can leave women vulnerable to further violence with little meaningful protection. For example, Human Rights Watch documented many cases in which Burundian women refugees were subjected to further beatings by their husbands or partners, after receiving counseling from the abashingatahe in the camps. Community-based mediation mechanisms, such as the abashingatahe, do not have the power to enforce their judgements or to punish perpetrators and thus deter them from committing further acts of physical violence against women. Hence, they should not be treated as an acceptable substitute for redress through the criminal justice system.

Through its research into the problem of domestic violence in a number of countries around the world, Human Rights Watch has found that the attitudes of law enforcement officials frequently serve the interests of the abuser, not those of the woman who is his victim. Women commonly face huge obstacles in seeking legal protection from domestic violence or in getting law enforcement authorities to take action against and prosecute their batterers and in obtaining protection from further violence. Laws against rape frequently exempt marital rape from criminal sanction; police refuse to take action against men who beat their wives and, in some cases, force women to withdraw complaints, or refuse to charge men with domestic assault, and women who seek restraining or protection orders are turned away by judicial authorities. In many countries, [28] judges readily accept "honor" or "heat

---

[28] For example, in Pakistan, Jordan, and South Africa. *See* Human Rights Watch reports: *Crime or Custom: Violence Against Women in Pakistan,* (New York: Human Rights Watch, August 1999); *Violence Against Women in South Africa* (New York: Human Rights Watch, November 1995); and *Human Rights Watch World Report 2000* (New York: Human Rights Watch: December 1999) pp.444-446. *See also,* "Jordan Parliament Supports Impunity for Honor Killing," (Washington, DC: Human Rights Watch Press Release, January 2000).

of passion" defenses by men who have murdered their wives, accepting a woman's adultery or other action as "legitimate provocation." Police and judicial authorities also dismiss domestic violence as a "private" matter rather than a crime that demands urgent state action. Women often experience severe violence in their homes, including rape, murder, assault, and battery—crimes that are prohibited by the criminal laws of virtually all countries. Yet when committed against a woman in an intimate relationship, these attacks are more often tolerated by law enforcement authorities as the norm than prosecuted as crimes, even when there are laws that specifically penalize domestic violence. In a number of countries, [29] those who commit domestic violence are prosecuted with less vigor and receive milder punishments than perpetrators of similarly violent crimes not committed in a domestic setting.

Refugee women who are subjected to domestic violence are often reluctant to invoke the laws of the host country to address this abuse.[30] They often face pressure from within their communities, and from their families and partners, not to report cases of domestic violence to the police. They may also feel intimidated and fear ostracization by their families and community, or retaliation from their abuser. They may still be emotionally attached to their abuser or be dependent on him for their and their children's welfare. At home, women victims usually turn to community mediation structures, although these may not be adequate to provide protection, especially in male dominated societies like that in Burundi. But even this option is often not possible in refugee settings, where there is typically an absence of consolidated community structures.

---

[29] For example, Russia, Peru, South Africa, and Pakistan. *See* Human Rights Watch reports: *Crime or Custom: Violence Against Women in Pakistan*, (New York: Human Rights Watch, August 1999); *Violence Against Women in South Africa* (New York: Human Rights Watch, November 1995); "Too Little, Too Late: State Response to Violence Against Women," (New York; Human Rights Watch, December 1997); and *Human Rights Watch World Report 2000* (New York: Human Rights Watch: December 1999) pp. 444 - 446. *See also* "Peru: Law of Protection from Family Violence," (New York: Human Rights Watch Memorandum, March 31, 2000).

[30] Radhika Coomaraswamy, U.N. Special Rapporteur on Violence Against Women report, "Violence Against Women, Its Causes and Consequences," (New York: United Nations Publications E\CN.4/1996/53, February 6, 1996).

Domestic Violence in Tanzanian Camps

Human Rights Watch identified high levels of domestic violence in the Tanzanian refugee camps in 1998 and 1999. Through firsthand research and from information obtained from humanitarian aid organizations working with the refugees, we found that a significant proportion of women had experienced repeated physical assaults by their husbands or intimate partners while living as refugees in the camps.[31] Victims had been assaulted with fists, bottles, shoes, sticks, and even machetes (*pangas*), and some had required hospitalization for their injuries. Many women interviewed by Human Rights Watch bore visible scars, bruises, or had broken fingers, missing teeth, or cuts on their faces and bodies. Some had suffered miscarriages or sexually transmitted diseases as a result of domestic sexual assault.[32] Yet, despite the seriousness and prevalence of domestic violence, neither UNHCR nor the Tanzanian host government had developed effective programs in response.[33]

The available statistics on the number of Burundian refugee women subjected to domestic violence are unreliable and, as our research suggests, significantly understate the problem, due to women's reluctance to report cases and to a lack of effective reporting mechanisms in the camps. Yet in the Kibondo camps, IRC

---

[31] Human Rights Watch interviews, project coordinator, IRC, Sexual and Gender-Based Violence Project, Kibondo, Tanzania, June 1, 1998; UNHCR consultant, Kasulu, Tanzania, May 26, 1998; community services officer, Christian Outreach, Kasulu, Tanzania, May 26, 1998; and community services officer, Dutch Relief Agency, Kibondo, Tanzania, June 3, 1998. Human Rights Watch interviewed community services officers from UNHCR and implementing partners Christian Outreach, Africare and Diocese of Western Tanganyika in the Kasulu camps; UMATI, Dutch Relief Agency, and IRC in the Kibondo camps; and Norwegian People's Aid in the Ngara camps on rates and statistics of domestic violence in the camps in October and November 1999. Although efforts are being made by these organizations to compile statistics, they are neither accurate nor conclusive of the rate of occurrence of domestic violence in the camps due to a variety of factors related to the nature of domestic violence. These include the ad hoc and cumbersome nature of collecting data on refugee violence, lack of reporting, and a lack of systematic follow-up of reported cases

[32] Human Rights Watch interviews, reproductive health officer, UNICEF, Kibondo, Tanzania, June 9, 1998 and reproductive health project assistant, UMATI Organization (an NGO that carries out research and provides health services to all refugees), Kibondo, Tanzania, June 9, 1998.

[33] This report does not attempt to examine all the causes of domestic violence in the refugee camps, but focuses more on recourse and particular preventative measures that UNHCR and implementing partners as well as the Tanzanian government must enforce in the camps.

documented 613[34] cases of domestic violence in 1998, in four camps: Kanembwa, Mkugwa, Mtendeli, and Nduta; and 764[35] cases in 1999.[36] UNHCR community services officers documented 321[37] cases of domestic violence in three camps in the Kasulu district: Nyarugusu, Mtabila, and Myovosi, between January and October 1999. [38] There were no records for the Kasulu camps for 1998 as UNHCR and community services and its implementing partners had not yet established programs to address domestic violence.[39] In the Ngara camps, Lukole A and B,[40] UNHCR community services and its implementing partner, Norwegian People's Aid, recorded forty-five cases of domestic violence between January and October 1999.[41]

Relationship between 1998 and 1999: Findings and Key Developments
    In 1998, when Human Rights Watch researchers visited Burundian refugee camps in Tanzania, they found a high incidence of domestic violence, specifically violence against women by their husbands or intimate partners. At that time, UNHCR and the Tanzanian authorities regarded such abuses as a "private" matter and took no action to intervene or afford the victims protection. Women victims of domestic violence had come neither to expect nor even to seek help from UNHCR or the Tanzanian authorities, and their abusers remained unpunished. Some Burundian women refugees told Human Rights Watch that they had learned to live with the problem of domestic violence, but others spoke compellingly of the feelings of fear and guilt that they experienced. In some cases, women said they had even come to

---

[34] Record of statistics drawn from IRC's monthly reports on Sexual and Gender-Based Violence Program given to Human Rights Watch by IRC reproductive health officer, IRC, New York, February 1999.

[35] Record of statistics drawn from IRC's monthly reports on Sexual and Gender-Based Violence Program given to Human Rights Watch by IRC's community services officers, Kibondo, Tanzania, November 9, 1999.

[36] As of January 2000, the total population in the Kibondo camps was approximately 171, 214 Burundians.

[37] Statistics drawn from UNHCR Sexual and Gender-Based Violence Program report received in November 3, 1999.

[38] As of February 2000, the total population in the Mtabila and Muyovosi camps was approximately 91,813 Burundians.

[39] Human Rights Watch interview, UNHCR community services consultant, Kasulu, Tanzania, May 24, 1998.

[40] As of January 2000, approximately 90,000 Burundian refugees lived in Lukole A and B camps.

[41] Human Rights Watch interview, UNHCR community services officer, Ngara, Tanzania, November 12, 1999.

feel responsible for violence perpetrated against them. Others expressed their dismay and devastation at being victimized twice: their lives had been disrupted due to the conflict in Burundi and then they had been subjected to another form of violence by their husbands in the camps. Some even said that they wished to return to Burundi, despite the conflict, to escape their violent husbands.[42]

When Human Rights Watch returned to the Tanzanian refugee camps in November 1999, there had been some marked and welcome developments. In particular, UNHCR had begun to give increased attention to the problem of domestic violence in the camps.[43] Since March 1999, UNHCR and its implementing partners had expanded their programs in the Kasulu camps to include domestic violence awareness campaigns and the provision of counseling for victims, as well as alternative plots on which to reside. Such services had not existed in 1998 except in the three Kibondo camps, where IRC had expanded its education and counseling program on sexual violence to include domestic violence.[44] In 1999, UNHCR expanded the education program on sexual and domestic violence initiated by IRC to all the other camps.

Refugee Camp Environment

Many Burundian women refugees were victims of domestic violence long before they fled their villages and towns and arrived in Tanzania,[45] but the special pressures, uncertainties, and indignities associated with their flight and the housing, security, food, and other problems which people tend to face in the camps can

---

[42] Although some refugees were not formally married, women and men alike used the term "husband" or "wife" to refer to their domestic partners, regardless of whether the union was sanctioned by the church or state.

[43] UNHCR community services and implementing partners coordinate a Sexual and Gender-Based Violence Program that addresses sexual and domestic violence in the Kasulu and Kibondo camps. In November 1999 when Human Rights Watch visited the Ngara camps , UNHCR's Sexual and Gender-Based Violence Program only addressed the problem of rape and other sexual crimes, but not domestic violence. The section on "Responses by UNHCR" has details on UNHCR's Sexual and Gender-Based Violence Program in the Tanzanian camps.

[44] Human Rights Watch interview, IRC coordinator, Sexual and Gender-Based Violence Program, Kibondo, Tanzania, June 1, 1998. The Section on "Responses by UNHCR" has details on IRC's programs in the Kibondo camps.

[45] Human Rights Watch interview, refugee women's forum (group of ninety-two women refugees attending a sewing club), Mtendeli camp, Tanzania, November 5, 1999.

exacerbate already frayed domestic situations, often leading to increased violence.[46] For example, the food distribution system which international relief agencies use in the camps can give rise to family disputes and, sometimes, violence. UNHCR ensures that each head of household, male or female, receives the food ration on behalf of their families. Male heads of household often act irresponsibly by selling food for cash or taking the food to their girlfriend or second family, leaving their wives and children with no food. Women reported that, when they questioned such behavior, they were beaten or threatened. Although women have the option to obtain their own ration cards, they are reluctant to do so, for fear of a husband's reaction.

UNHCR has made several adjustments to the food distribution systems in the camps to include more women on the food committees, and will issue ration cards in a woman's name upon her request. However, many women are unaware of this until they are already victims of domestic violence and are receiving counseling from UNHCR staff or its implementing partners' staff. But even issuing ration cards in women's names does not guarantee that they can control what happens to their family's ration within their household, and some of it may be sold on by their husbands.

Not surprisingly, many refugee men feel that aspects of life in the camps challenge their traditional male role in Burundian society. In particular, male refugees complain that their role and standing in the home is effectively being usurped by UNHCR. As one man put it, "UNHCR now provides housing for my family, food for my kids, and clothing for my wife. What use am I any more?"[47] This challenge to their traditional role as providers for their families tends to lead to anger, frustration, uncertainty, and helplessness among male refugees, and sometimes this translates into violence against women in the refugee camps.[48]

Other social pressures also contribute to tension between couples and violence in the camps. For example, polygamy is illegal in Burundi, a Catholic country, except in a few small Muslim enclaves. In some cases, however, Burundian men left families behind in Burundi when they fled to Tanzania, took a new wife and started a new family in the refugee camp, only for their first wife and family then

---

[46] Human Rights Watch interviews, refugee women representatives, Mtabila 1 and 2, Kanembwa, Mtendeli, and Nduta camps; and refugee crisis intervention team, Lukole A and B camps, Tanzania, October and November 1999

[47] Human Rights Watch interview, sungu-sungus, Nduta camp, November 8, 1999. *See also*, UNHCR, *Angry Young Men in Camps: Gender, Age, Class Relations among Burundian Refugees in Tanzania* (UNHCR, Geneva, June 1999).

[48] Ibid.

to arrive from Burundi. In other cases, male refugees have taken openly a second or a third wife within the camps and started new families alongside their existing ones, and this has added to tensions. Some men we interviewed openly admitted to having taken additional wives in the camp.

Within the Tanzanian refugee camps, systems that women relied upon to help address domestic violence when they lived in Burundi—extended networks of family, neighbors, and community leaders—still exist, but in a much weaker, more compromised and less reliable form. Consequently, battered women are often left destitute with few means to seek protection or hide from their abusers, and perpetrators are often left free and unpunished—due to a lack of effective legal mechanisms and women victims' own reluctance to report their abusers to the police—and can further beat or torment their victims with virtual impunity.

Nature of the Response

The responsibility for protecting refugees lies with both the host government and UNHCR, and there is a clear need for UNHCR and the Tanzanian government to take much more concerted action to halt, punish, and prevent domestic violence from occurring. Currently, however, Tanzania's law enforcement mechanisms are almost non-functional, particularly with regard to investigating and prosecuting cases of domestic violence, due both to resource problems and to discriminatory attitudes among law enforcement officers and police.[49] Also, among refugees themselves, there is enormous resistance to relying on outsiders to resolve domestic disputes. In general, refugees prefer community-based mechanisms to the host country's courts in resolving domestic violence, as the former are run by other refugees and focus more on counseling and reconciliation.[50]

There are many community-based mediation mechanisms in the Tanzanian refugee camps, from abashingatahe to women representatives, to elderly women and church leaders. The abashingatahe are mostly male refugees, although UNHCR has ensured that a few women are also able to play this role. Male abashingatahe often

---

[49] *See* section on "Responses by the Tanzanian Government" for details on police attitudes to domestic violence. There is, however, hope for change as a new security contingent of about 258 Tanzanian police was deployed to the refugee camps in September and November 1999. UNHCR planned to initiate training programs on police responsibilities in refugee operations, including police attitudes to crimes such as domestic and sexual violence committed mostly against women.

[50] Human Rights Watch interviews, refugee women representatives, Mtabila 1 and 2, Kanembwa, Mtendeli, and Nduta camps and refugee crisis intervention team, Lukole A and B camps, Tanzania, October and November 1999.

hold many of the same sexist attitudes toward women as the men they judge. Furthermore, the abashingatahe are susceptible to corruption and have no enforcement powers. Sometimes, instead of providing redress, they effectively blame women victims for the abuse they have suffered, and tell them that, in the future, they should avoid improper behavior that will result in their husbands beating them.

Cases of Domestic Violence

In May and June 1998, Human Rights Watch interviewed twenty Burundian women refugees who had been beaten by their husbands while in the Mtendeli, Kanembwa, Nduta, and Mtabila camps. We spoke to twenty-five more women victims in October and November 1999. In addition, Human Rights Watch conducted dozens of group interviews with both female and male refugee leaders in each camp visited during the 1998 and 1999 missions. Women refugees told harrowing stories of repeated assaults and suffering. Some of their testimonies are recorded below. These testimonies point to various aspects of the problem—how severely some women victims are injured; the failure of police to investigate adequately or to arrest perpetrators of domestic violence; and the absence of effective community-based mechanisms to safeguard women refugees in the camps from domestic violence.

Failure of the Police to Intervene

Soplange S.[51] sustained a deep cut on her forehead and bruises all over her body when her husband beat her with a stick in 1998. Thirty years old, she is married with four children. She fled to Tanzania in early 1996 with her family. Since her second month in Kanembwa camp, her husband had beaten her regularly, often more than twice a week. Then on May 30, 1998, her husband came home late and very drunk, entered the room where she was sleeping, and started beating her. She screamed for help and was heard by the neighbors, but they did not intervene for fear of her husband. When Human Rights Watch interviewed her, she had fled from her home and was staying with her brother, also a refugee in Kanembwa camp, and was being treated for her injuries at the camp hospital. She had reported the assault to the police, but they had not arrested her husband.[52]

---

[51] Unless otherwise noted, all names have been changed, and the ages given reflect the age of the person at the time of the interview.

[52] Human Rights Watch interview, Soplange S., Kanembwa camp, Tanzania, June 3, 1998.

Rosalie P.'s teeth were knocked out when her husband hit her head against a tree, and her face was still bruised when Human Rights Watch interviewed her in June 1998. A twenty-seven-year-old, she had arrived in Tanzania in 1997 and married her husband in Mtendeli camp. Soon after, in January 1998, he began an extra-marital affair. He beat Rosalie P. on May 28, 1998, after she refused to prepare a meal for the other woman. Rosalie P. had reported the case to the police but they had not arrested her husband.[53]

Thirty-nine-year-old Gaudencia T. began experiencing domestic violence in 1997 after her husband had an affair with another woman in Mtendeli camp. She, her husband, and two children fled to Tanzania in 1996 and settled in Mtendeli camp. In May 1998, her husband went out one day and did not come back until the next morning. Gaudencia T. was afraid to ask him where he had slept for fear of angering him, but he then beat her because she did not ask him where he had been. When interviewed by Human Rights Watch, her upper lip was badly bruised and her eyes were swollen. She stated:

> My husband beat me and insulted me using vulgar and obscene language about my body. He compared my body to other women's whom he had before, and this was in the presence of our children. After beating me, he forced me to have sex with him. I did not report this case to the police because in the past they have not arrested him after I reported similar incidents.[54]

The failure of the Tanzanian police to investigate cases was continuing when Human Rights Watch returned to the camps in 1999. Munzime P. stated that she had sustained a broken finger when her husband beat her in 1999, but the police did not arrest her husband when she reported the assault. Aged twenty- four, she has two children and fled Burundi in 1994, staying in Mtabila camp until January 1999, when she moved to Nduta camp. She said her husband had beaten her in September 1999:

> My husband beat me severely on September 29, 1999. The problem started at night when he insulted me about my illness. I have an epileptic problem. On that day, I had an epileptic attack and I could not have sex

---

[53] Human Rights Watch interview, Rosalie P., Mtendeli camp, Tanzania, June 7, 1998.

[54] Human Rights Watch interview, Gaudencia T., Mtendeli camp, Tanzania, June 7, 1998.

with him. My husband started shouting at me using abusive language, calling me an ugly and useless woman. He twisted my fingers till one got dislocated. He kicked me several times on my face and stomach. I could not cry for help because he was threatening to kill me if I cried out. On the following day, I reported the case to the sungu- sungus but they did not intervene to punish my husband, because he gave them money. I also reported the case to the police, but they did not arrest him. In October 1999, my husband fled from Nduta camp, and I do not know where he is now. I wanted my husband to be arrested and punished for beating me when I was ill. Since my husband left, there is nobody to help me look after the children. When my husband left Nduta camp, he took all the food and non-food items and left me with nothing. In November 1999, the Dutch Relief Agency[55] gave me some cooking pots, blankets, and plastic sheets.[56]

In some cases, victims of domestic violence are intimidated by their husbands into not reporting their cases to the police. Monique V. suffered severe injuries at the hands of her husband, but she did not report the case to the police because she was afraid of her husband. Monique V., age seventeen, had fled to Tanzania with her parents in 1997 and married another refugee whom she met in Mtendeli camp in January 1998. He beat her when she was pregnant, so she went back to her parents in Kanembwa camp, but they always told her to return to her husband. She said the neighbors had witnessed her being beaten several times and had rescued her, but they regarded her with shame. She stated:

On May 1, 1998, my husband kicked me several times in the stomach. At that time, I was four months pregnant. I was hospitalized for four weeks and miscarried. I did not report the case to the police because I was afraid of my husband.[57]

---

[55] Dutch Relief Agency is a humanitarian organization that provides services to refugees, such as material support, community-based education programs, and counseling to victims of abuse in the camps, particularly women and girls who have experienced sexual and domestic violence.

[56] Human Rights Watch interview, Munzime P., Nduta camp, Tanzania, November 8, 1999.

[57] Human Rights Watch interview, Monique V., Mtendeli camp, Tanzania, June 7, 1998.

Bezisiriya S. was threatened and intimidated by her husband to prevent her from reporting him to the police or UNHCR staff for beating her. She came to Mtendeli camp in 1996 with her husband and two children and, when Human Rights Watch interviewed her in November 1999, was twenty-two years old. She said her relations with her husband had deteriorated when she complained about him selling some of the family's ration food at the local market in June 1999, leaving nothing for her and the children. Since August 1999, he had refused to have sex with her, and when he learned that Bezisiriya S. had complained to her aunt about this, he had beaten her severely. Bezisiriya S. told Human Rights Watch:

On October 15,1999, my aunt, who is also living in Mtendeli camp, came to our plot to counsel my husband about his refusal to have sex with me. My husband got very angry with me for reporting him to my aunt, and as soon as my aunt left, he beat me severely with a stick. I bled through the nose and mouth, but he continued to kick me even as I was bleeding. He denied me permission to go to hospital for treatment. He also denied me permission to leave the house or to interact with other refugee women in the camp. I am afraid that, if he finds out that I left the house today, he will kill me because he threatened to do so if ever he discovered that I had reported him to the police or the camp authorities. I have not reported the case to anybody because I am afraid of my husband.[58]

Radegonde L. was also threatened and intimidated by her husband, and too frightened to report his assaults on her to the police. An eighteen-year-old married woman, she fled to Tanzania with her parents in 1994 and lived with them in Kanembwa camp until she married in 1997 and moved to Mtendeli camp with her husband. She said that he beat her because she had not become pregnant since they were married. On June 1, 1998, he locked the door of their house and then beat and verbally abused her for not becoming pregnant. She was unable to escape or call for help, as he had held her mouth closed tightly with his hand. Radegonde L. stated:

My husband only stopped beating me when I was seriously injured. My nose and mouth were bleeding. He took me to the hospital, where I stayed

---

[58] Human Rights Watch interview, Bezisiriya S., Mtendeli camp, Tanzania, November 5, 1999.

for two weeks. I did not report the case to the police because my husband threatened to kill me if I reported him.[59]

Reconciliatory Counseling not Enough

Despite the counseling provided by UNHCR community services officers or its implementing partners, the involvement of abashingatahe, women representatives, sungu-sungus, and others, victims of domestic violence told Human Rights Watch that such measures only had a temporary effect, and many men continued beating their wives regardless of any intervention. For example, Herapile T., a twenty-two-year-old woman living in Nduta camp, said that her husband had beaten her several times since 1998, despite the warnings and counseling he had received. She told Human Rights Watch:

> After we got married in November 1998, my husband started telling me that other refugees were mocking and laughing at him about my physical appearance. He told me that I am very ugly and dark and he was thinking of finding a fair wife. Afterwards, the story changed and my husband started accusing me of having a boyfriend in the camp. Since May 1999, my husband has been beating me, even more than six times a week. He used his hands to beat me. We were counseled by several people, including sungu-sungus, women representatives, and even the block leaders and abashingatahe, but my husband continued to beat me. In August 1999, the block leader counseled us, but my husband beat me again on the same day after we had been counseled. During the second week of October, he beat me severely after demanding that he wanted me to give birth to a baby boy. I was three months pregnant. He kicked me several times in the stomach. My neighbors took me to hospital. I was hospitalized and had a miscarriage four days later. I stayed in the hospital for two weeks receiving treatment. I reported the case to the Dutch Relief Agency, and they counseled me and assisted me with food and non-food items. I have not had any problems with my husband since we separated in November 1999. I was given my own plot by UNHCR in November

---

[59] Human Rights Watch interview, Radegonde L., Mtendeli camp, Tanzania, June 7, 1998.

1999. I did not report the case to the police because other refugees in the camp discouraged me from doing so.[60]

Jeanne Y. is another woman refugee whose husband had beaten her despite warnings from the abashingatahe. A thirty-year-old mother of five children, she and her family fled to Tanzania in November 1996 and settled in Mtendeli camp. While there, she had three miscarriages, and a fourth pregnancy ended with the child dying soon after delivery. She said that her husband began to beat her when she did not become pregnant again. On May 31, 1998, her husband beat her after drinking beer, causing her serious head and ear injuries which required her to spend two weeks in the camp hospital. She reported the beating to the abashingatahe, who warned her husband but took no other action. After leaving the hospital, she went back to live with her husband, even though he continued to beat her.[61]

Sale of Ration Food

UNHCR does not have a policy that specifies who is to receive family food rations, but food ration cards, in practice, are issued to male heads of household and not to their wives. Ration cards are issued to women only when there is no male head of household or if they are single and unaccompanied.

As a result, some battered refugee women continue to live with their abusers because they fear losing access to their food rations. Others told Human Rights Watch that they feared requesting food ration cards in their own names and separate shelter because this could result in more violence by their husbands. Others who had made such requests in 1998 complained that it had taken UNHCR over a month to respond while they were living in fear that their abusers would find out.

In 1999, UNHCR initiated a new food distribution system that increases women's visibility in key leadership positions in the camps and secures greater female participation in the process of food distribution. However, this helps only to ensure that refugee families receive the precise rations due to them. UNHCR had not tackled the more difficult task of preventing male members of the household from selling some of the food for cash or alcohol or passing it out to another woman

---

[60] Human Rights Watch interview, Herapile T., Nduta camp, Tanzania, November 8, 1999.

[61] Human Rights Watch interview, Jeanne Y., Mtendeli camp, Tanzania, June 7, 1998.

and her family, leaving their own wives and children hungry.[62] When Human Rights Watch raised this issue with UNHCR field officers who are responsible for the management of food distribution, their response was that it would be difficult for UNHCR to control the use of food once it reaches households.[63] A field officer in Kibondo said, "We try to follow up cases in which women report that their husbands sell or mismanage the food, and we give the ration food directly to the woman in such cases. In some of the cases our strategy works while in others, the problem persists."[64] For example, Beatrice F., aged twenty-two and married with two children, told Human Rights Watch that her husband began to sell half of the family's food in early 1999, and then spend the money he got in return on beer. When Beatrice F. complained, she said, he beat her severely. When interviewed by Human Rights Watch, she bore bruises on her face and neck caused, she said, by a beating from her husband the previous night. She had not reported the problem to UNHCR or the camp authorities because she feared her husband. Nor had she applied for her own ration card and separate plot on which to reside, because her husband had threatened to kill her if she did. She said that she was so desperate that she was even thinking of returning to Burundi to escape the beatings and threats from her husband.[65]

Annette G. fled to Tanzania in 1996 with her husband and three children, and was twenty-five years old when Human Rights Watch interviewed her. She was then living with her family in Kanembwa camp, though her husband had beaten her frequently since they arrived in Tanzania. He sold all the family's food given by UNHCR and spent the money on beer, and beat her when she protested this. He beat her in front of the children the day before Human Rights Watch met her: she had bruises all over her body. He had been warned by refugee leaders to stop the beatings, but had ignored this, boasting that he would continue. Annette G. said

---

[62] Human Rights Watch interview, women representatives, Mtabila 1 and 2 camps, Tanzania, November 1, 1999; women representatives, Kanembwa camp, Tanzania, November 6, 1999; women's forum, Mtendeli camp, Tanzania, November 5, 1999; and women representatives, Nduta camp, Tanzania, November 8, 1999.

[63] Human Rights Watch interviews, UNHCR Field Officers, Kibondo, Tanzania, November 8, 1999.

[64] Ibid

[65] Human Rights Watch interview, Beatrice F., Mtendeli camp, Tanzania, November 5, 1999.

that she no longer reported beatings to the police because they were uninterested on previous occasions.[66]

Thirty-three-year-old Virginie M. had been waiting for a ration card for over three weeks when Human Rights Watch interviewed her in June 1998. She arrived in Tanzania in 1996. Her husband, she said, beat her frequently and had threatened to slit her throat. She was then living with another woman refugee, having fled from her husband's abuse. She wanted her husband to be arrested and prosecuted, but the police at Nduta camp had refused to take action against him because, she said, a senior police officer there was one of her husband's friends. She had requested her own ration card, but not a separate living plot because she feared her husband would attack her again if he learned where she was staying.[67]

Status of Women and Other Social Problems

In their interviews with Human Rights Watch, Burundian women refugees indicated that all manner of petty issues could lead to their being assaulted in their homes by their husbands or partners. These issues ranged from not having a meal prepared at the right time or not having meat for a meal, to protesting against their husband's misbehavior in selling part of the family's food ration, engaging in an extramarital affair, or getting drunk. Other problems associated with life in a refugee camp, including enforced idleness, poverty, and frustration, clearly are factors which add to the pressures on families and contribute to a high occurrence of domestic violence.

Refugees complained that living in the artificial refugee camp environments tended to erode their cultural values. For example, many married Burundian male refugees effectively entered into polygamous relationships, although in Burundi itself polygamy is strictly prohibited.[68] Many others had extramarital affairs. This behavior by refugee men often generated tension and violence between married

---

[66] Human Rights Watch interview, Annette G., Kanembwa Camp, Tanzania, June 3, 1998.

[67] Human Rights Watch interview, Virginie M., Nduta camp, Tanzania, June 6, 1998.

[68] Human Rights Watch interviews, abashingatahe, Mtabila 1 and 2 camps, Tanzania, November 2, 1999; women representatives, Mtabila 1 and 2 camps, Tanzania, November 1, 1999; sungu-sungus, Mtabila 1 and 2 camps, Tanzania, November 2, 1999; sungu-sungus, Kanembwa camp, Tanzania, November 4, 1999; abashingatahe, Kanembwa camp, Tanzania, November 6, 1999; women representatives, Kanembwa camp, Tanzania, November 6, 1999; sungu sungus, Mtendeli camp, Tanzania, November 5, 1999; and women's forum, Mtendeli camp, Tanzania, November 5, 1999.

couples.[69] Anina D., a twenty-five-year-old mother of one child, told Human Rights Watch that her husband began to beat her in 1998 after he took a girlfriend in Nduta camp. He had then given her clothes to his girlfriend, leading Anina D. to report this to IRC's community services officers. They then asked her husband to come and see them but, instead, he fled Nduta camp with his girlfriend after first beating up his wife and taking all the family's food and possessions with him, leaving her with nothing. Anina D. told Human Rights Watch:

> I sustained bruises on the face and neck from the injury. He threatened that he was going to ambush and kill me, because he had found a more beautiful wife. I reported the case to the police who in turn referred me back to the refugee leaders for assistance. I wanted the police to investigate the case and arrest my husband because I am afraid he might return to kill me as he threatened on the day he fled from Nduta camp. I have been assisted by IRC with counseling, and the Dutch Relief Agency gave me some non-food items.[70]

Epiphanie B., a forty-two-year old mother of three children, was also beaten up by her husband when a woman with whom he had previously had an extramarital relationship before their flight from Burundi also arrived in Tanzania and settled at Nduta camp. Epiphanie B.'s husband took their food and property and gave it to this other woman and then beat Epiphanie B. with sticks and his fists when she protested. The other woman joined him in the assault. Epiphanie B. sustained a head injury and was forced to leave home and move in with another woman refugee. She wanted her husband and his girlfriend to be punished but the local police appeared uninterested in her plight:

> My husband threw me and our three children off the plot of land where we lived. He now lives on that plot with his girlfriend, and I have nowhere to stay with the children. I reported the case to the police, and they did nothing to help me. I also reported the case to UNHCR and requested a plot

---

[69] Refugee men also complained to Human Rights Watch that married women were having boyfriends or extra-marital relationships in the camps.

[70] Human Rights Watch interview, Anina D., Nduta camp, Tanzania, November 8, 1998.

and separate ration card. UNHCR has not yet responded to my requests. I made the requests four weeks ago.[71]

Sara D., a nineteen-year-old with a six-month-old child, had lived in Mtendeli camp since around December 1996 and married her husband there in March 1998. But, she said, their marriage had been peaceful for only five months. Then her husband started beating her and threatening to take another wife, and the violence intensified when she became pregnant and asked him to purchase cloth for her to make maternity clothes. He beat her for that and she left him and returned to her parent's home several times. However, her husband had local clergy talk to her and convince her to return to him, which she had done because she feared what would happen to her as a single mother, in the camp. UNHCR then intervened to help her recover her belongings, by holding on to her husband's ration card until he returned them. She said he beat her because she had refused to have their baby registered on his ration card and for other reasons.[72]

Human Rights Watch interviewed Rebecca N., a twenty-eight-year-old divorced mother of a four-year-old child, at Mtendeli camp. She said she had married a man there because she felt the need for protection, as women were being raped at the camp and when they left the camps to collect firewood. But the man she married turned out to have a wife in Burundi, and, when his first wife arrived in Tanzania, he began to abuse verbally, threaten, and insult Rebecca N. and asked her for a divorce. Because his first wife's sister worked for one of the humanitarian organizations in the camp, they ensured that Rebecca N. was quickly given her own ration card and relocated to a different house.[73]

Safe Shelters

Governments and private organizations in a number of countries around the world have established special shelters and places of refuge for women who are victims of domestic violence and their children. Usually these are run by non-governmental organizations with total or partial government funding. They

---

[71] Human Rights Watch interview, Epiphanie B., Nduta camp, Tanzania, June 3, 1998. Most Burundian refugees interviewed by Human Rights Watch used the term "second wife" when referring to the girlfriend of a married Burundian man. Polygamy is not legal under Burundian law; hence the term "girlfriend" has been used in this report to refer to a woman who has a relationship with a married man.

[72] Human Rights Watch interview, Sara D., Mtendeli camp, Kibondo district, November 5, 1999.

[73] Human Rights Watch interview, Rebecca N., Mtendeli camp, November 5, 1999.

frequently provide a safe and private environment in which victims of domestic violence are safeguarded against further abuse and can begin to try to recover from the trauma to which they have been exposed, and they are not run for profit.[74]

As yet, insufficient research has been undertaken to determine the viability of establishing such shelters in refugee camps, but there is a clear need to provide some form of safe haven for victims of domestic violence, and this is recognized by UNHCR and humanitarian organizations working with the Burundian refugees in Tanzania.[75] There is some fear, of course, that safe shelters could become targets for attacks by disgruntled spouses or others, and would be especially vulnerable when situated within large refugee camps. Lacking such shelters, women victims of domestic violence in the Tanzanian camps said they often seek help from their network of relatives and friends, with abused women looking to other, sympathetic refugees to give them temporary shelter in their own homes and to share their small food rations with them. Since August 1999, however, the IRC Sexual and Gender-Based Violence Project has provided temporary shelter at its drop-in centers in the Kibondo camps and were looking into possibilities to construct permanent shelters for women victims of violence in the Mtendeli and Nduta camps.[76]

---

[74] Rhadhika Coomaraswamy, U.N. Special Rapporteur on Violence Against Women report, "Violence Against Women, Its Causes and Consequences," (New York: United Nations Publications E\CN.4/1996/53, February 6, 1996), p. 138.

[75] Human Rights Watch interviews, senior reproductive health officer, UNHCR, Kibondo, Tanzania, November 7, 1999; community services officer, UNHCR, Kasulu, Tanzania, November 2, 1999; IRC community services officers, November 6, 199; and Dutch relief Agency community services officers, Kibondo, Tanzania, November 6, 1999.

[76] Human Rights Watch interview, IRC community services officers, Kibondo, Tanzania, November 6, 1999. Also see the sections on "Sexual Violence" for details on IRC's drop-in centers and on "Responses by UNHCR" for details on IRC's efforts to establish shelters.

V. SEXUAL VIOLENCE

Scope of the Problem

In many areas of the world, refugee women flee conflict after having been terrorized with rape and other sexual and physical abuse. Yet seeking to escape these dangers, many are then subjected to similar abuse as refugees.[77] Refugee and internally displaced women worldwide have recounted harrowing stories of abuse and suffering, including rape and other sexual assaults.[78]

Within refugee camps, women refugees may be subjected to rape because of their increased vulnerability as refugees, or because of their actual or perceived political or ethnic affiliations. Rape and other forms of sexual assault are frequently gender-specific not only in their form but also in their motivation. Thus, refugee women and girls are raped because of their gender, irrespective of their age, ethnicity, or political beliefs. In host countries, local residents, military and immigration officials, and police, often view refugee women as easy targets for assault. Fellow refugees also target refugee women for sexual violence.

The injuries that refugee women sustain from being raped persist long after the crime. Refugee women interviewed by Human Rights Watch in different parts of the world have reported ongoing medical problems, including psychological trauma, miscarriages by women raped when pregnant, hemorrhaging for long periods, inability to control urination, sleeplessness, nightmares, chest and back pains, and painful menstruation.[79]

The strong cultural stigma attached to rape further intensifies the rape victims' physical and psychological trauma. Women in refugee camps and those who are internally displaced who acknowledge being raped may be ostracized, or even punished, by their families. As a result, women survivors of sexual violence often are reluctant to seek medical assistance or to file police reports because they do not want it known that they were raped. Even when incidents are reported, however,

---

[77] *See* "Sexual Assault of Refugee and Displaced Women," in Human Rights Watch, *The Human Rights Watch Global Report on Women's Human Rights* (New York: Human Rights Watch, August 1995) pp. 100-139.

[78] *See e.g.*, Human Rights Watch, "Afghanistan: The Massacre in Mazar-I Sharif,"(New York: Human Rights Watch, November 1998.); Human Rights Watch, "*Sierra Leone: Getting away with Murder, Mutilation, and Rape*," (New York: Human Rights Watch, June 1999.); Human Rights Watch, *Burundi: Proxy Targets: Civilians in the War*, (New York: Human Rights Watch, March 1998.); and Human Rights Watch, *2000 World Report*, (New York: Human Rights Watch, December 1999.)

[79] *Global Report on Women's Human Rights*, p. 42.

effective responses may not be forthcoming, since international humanitarian organizations, as well as countries of asylum, often ignore or are not adequately trained and equipped to handle reports of rape and other sexual crimes.

Rape in the Tanzanian Camps

Human Rights Watch found that Burundian refugee women living in the Tanzanian camps have been raped by other Burundian refugees and by Tanzanians from nearby villages. Our research in 1998 and 1999 found that women were often attacked while carrying out routine daily tasks such as gathering firewood, collecting vegetables, farming, or seeking employment from local Tanzanian villagers. Increased tension between refugees and Tanzanians who live near refugee settlements sometimes results in physical attacks on refugees and sexual attacks on women. Tanzanian authorities and villagers in western Tanzania increasingly view refugees as a threat to their security.[80] As reported above, in a particularly serious incident in May 1999, some fifty or more refugee women were raped by over 100 Tanzanian men in Kasulu district, but only eleven men had been arrested by November 1999[81] and were being held at Kasulu prison, awaiting prosecution.[82] All eleven defendants were brought for trial before a court in Kasulu town on December 15, 1999. However, the judge dismissed the case because the prosecutor was late to appear in court, and all the defendants were released.[83] The women victims were being counseled by UNHCR community services and implementing partners.[84]

---

[80] Human Rights Watch interview, Tanzania Officials, MHA, Dar-es-Salaam, Tanzania, November 16, 1999.

[81] Human Rights Watch interviews, UNHCR protection officer, Kasulu, Tanzania, October 31, 1999 and magistrate, Kasulu district court, Tanzania, November 2, 1999. We did not get information on the final outcomes of these cases. Also, *see* Human Rights Watch, *World Report 2000* (New York: Human Rights Watch, November 1999), p 440.

[82] Human Rights Watch interview, magistrate, Kasulu district court, Tanzania, November 2, 1999.

[83] Section 222 of the Tanzanian Code of Criminal Procedure provides that a judge has the option to dismiss a case if the prosecutor fails to arrive, or to defer it if it is deemed to be in the best interests of justice. *See also* Amnesty International, "Refugees Denied Protection," (London: Amnesty International, May 2000) p. 8.

[84] Human Rights Watch interview, UNHCR community services officer, Kasulu, Tanzania, November 2, 1999.

According to UNHCR officials in Kasulu, although fifty women came forward to report the rapes, the actual number of victims may have been higher.[85]

Statistics on rape of women refugees in Tanzania are unreliable, and many victims of rape are thought never to report their cases to UNHCR, camp authorities, or the police given the stigma attached to rape, their fear of the authorities, or because of what they perceive as the latter's discriminatory or unsympathetic attitudes. Burundian women refugees said they sometimes remained silent after suffering rape in order to avoid bringing shame and humiliation on themselves, or being blamed by their families and communities. Some said they faced hostility, rejection, and even violence from their husbands, or others in the community, if they reported instances of sexual abuse to which they had been subjected. Some women victims of rape complained that their husbands blamed them for the rapes and beat them for having been raped.

Some rape victims Human Rights Watch interviewed in 1998 complained of the lack of effective protection and preventive mechanisms,[86] and of perpetrators effectively benefiting from impunity. At that time, neither UNHCR nor the Tanzanian government had developed tangible programs to combat rape in the camps, and apparently Tanzanian police officers often demanded bribes from victims before they would investigate or simply blamed the victims for the crimes.[87] Only in the Kibondo camps was there a program in place to raise awareness among refugees about the problem of sexual violence and to counsel victims, this having been initiated by IRC in 1996.[88]

In the Kasulu camps, Mtabila and Muyovosi, refugee women's representatives told Human Rights Watch in 1998 that there was a high level of sexual violence,

---

[85] Human Rights Watch interview, UNHCR protection officer, Kasulu, Tanzania, October 31, 1999.

[86] Preventative measures may include education and awareness campaigns for all refugees about the problem of rape, escorting women when they travel outside the camps to collect firewood, and placing police on patrol areas where women go to collect firewood.

[87] *See* section on "Responses by the Tanzanian Government" for details on the inadequacies of the Tanzanian government law enforcement.

[88] *See* section on "Responses by UNHCR" for details on IRC's program of response to sexual and gender-based violence in the Kibondo camps.

especially against young girls,[89] but that many cases were not being reported.[90] Twelve cases of rape were reported to UNHCR by refugees in the Mtabila, Muyovosi, and Nyarugusu camps between January and May 1998, all committed by other refugees, sometimes by boys as young as fourteen and sixteen years. By May 1998, six of the alleged culprits were being prosecuted in the local courts.[91]

In the Ngara camps, Lukole A and B, where there were then no concrete programs to raise community awareness about sexual violence, twenty-seven cases of rape were reported to UNHCR throughout 1998. But women refugees told Human Rights Watch that rape victims often had little or no information about what to do or where to go to report their cases.[92] At the Ngara camps in June 1998, most rapes of women refugees occurred when they left the confines of their camp to look for firewood and became victims of other refugees, local Tanzanian men, or Rwandans. These latter, they said, included members of the *interahamwe* militia involved in the 1994 Rwandan genocide,[93] while others were Rwandan refugees who had become refugees after evading the Tanzanian army when it forced half a million Rwandan refugees back into Rwanda in 1996. These bandits were said to have abducted young Burundian refugee women from the camps in Ngara for sex and forced labor.[94]

Documentation by IRC in 1997 and 1998 revealed a high level of sexual violence. In the Kibondo camps, where IRC had begun a program to raise

---

[89] Human Rights Watch interview, women's representatives, Muyovosi camp, Tanzania, May 28, 1998.

[90] Human Rights Watch interview, UNHCR community services consultant, Kasulu district, Tanzania, May 26, 1998.

[91] Human Rights Watch interview, UNHCR assistant protection officer, Kasulu, Tanzania, May 27, 1998.

[92] Human Rights Watch interview, refugee women representatives, Lukole A and B camps, Tanzania, June 6, 1998.

[93] "Interahamwe" was the Kinyarwanda (a Rwandan language) name for the mostly Hutu militia that carried out the 1994 genocide of Tutsi in Rwanda. It is now loosely used to refer to insurgents against the Rwandan government, whether or not they actually participated in the genocide. For a history of the Rwandan genocide, *see* Human Rights Watch, *Leave None To Tell The Story: Genocide in Rwanda* (New York: Human Rights Watch, March 1999); for the use of rape in the genocide, *see* Human Rights Watch, *Shattered Lives: Sexual Violence during the Rwandan Genocide and its Aftermath* (New York: Human Rights Watch, September 1996).

[94] Human Rights Watch interview, refugee security guardians, Ngara, Tanzania, June 7, 1998.

community awareness on sexual violence, IRC documented 122 cases of rape between January and December 1998.[95] When IRC set up a community-based program for refugee women in Kanembwa camp in October 1996, sixty-eight women and children came forward within two months to report cases of rape, domestic violence, and child abuse, including rape of children.[96] In September 1997, IRC published a report that provided alarming information about sexual violence against Burundian women refugees in Kanembwa camp, where it maintains one of its drop-in centers, indicating, on the basis of a survey carried out in the camp in which some 3,800 women were interviewed, that approximately 26 percent of girls and women in the twelve to forty-nine age range reported having been subjected to violence either during flight from Burundi or while in the camp.

In some cases, efforts to follow up on the status or outcomes of rape cases occurring in the camps in 1998 were frustrated by a lack of comprehensive reporting mechanisms. Neither the Tanzanian police nor UNHCR officers maintained clear records of reported cases of rape in the camps in 1998. In some cases, obtaining further information on cases was hindered by a variety of factors: either the victim was no longer living in the same camp, the perpetrator was at large, or the investigating officer was no longer attached to the refugee camp, and there was no record of the case.

Relationship Between 1998 and 1999: Findings and Key Developments

When Human Rights Watch returned to the Tanzanian refugee camps in 1999, it was clear that UNHCR's response to rape had improved. UNHCR protection officers maintained better records of rape cases, reported the incidence of rape in each camp, and more closely monitored those cases referred for prosecution. By November 1999, UNHCR had referred fifteen rape cases from the four Kibondo camps—Kanembwa, Mtendeli, Nduta, and Mkugwa—to the Kibondo district court for prosecution since the beginning of 1999,[97] and three of these had resulted in the conviction and imprisonment of the rapists. Eight other accused were awaiting trial, and four had been discharged, either because a witness had failed to appear or due

---

[95] Human Rights Watch E-mail from IRC reproductive health officer, IRC, New York, March 18, 1999.

[96] IRC, "Pain Too Deep For Tears: Assessing the Prevalence of Sexual and Gender Violence Among Burundian Refugees in Tanzania," (New York: International Rescue Committee, September 1997).

[97] Statistics given to Human Rights Watch by UNHCR Sexual and Gender-Based project lawyer, Kibondo, Tanzania, November 9, 1999.

to a lack of sufficient evidence.[98] From the Kasulu camps, Mtabila 1 and 2, Muyovosi, and Nyarugusu, UNHCR referred forty rape cases to the Kasulu district court.[99]

Other humanitarian organizations also compiled information on gender-related offenses in the camps.[100] Norwegian People's Aid (NPA), for example, UNHCR's main implementing partner responsible for sexual and gender-based violence programs in the Lukole A and B camps, recorded twenty-four rapes and forty-five cases of domestic violence from January to October 1999.[101] IRC documented 111 cases of rape in the four Kibondo camps over the same period.[102] In 1999, programs to raise community awareness of sexual violence and to provide counseling to rape victims were established in all the camps. These programs are mostly run by UNHCR, community services implementing partners, and other NGOs.

In 1999, UNHCR also began to give greater attention and judicial access to, as well as redress for, victims of rape, which had not been the case in 1998. In September 1999, UNHCR recruited two women lawyers to assist women rape victims and provide legal advice, and to follow up on cases of rape and other crimes committed against refugee women that are referred to the courts. In the Ngara camps, where UNHCR had not yet recruited a lawyer to assist women in pursuing their cases in court, Human Rights Watch was told by UNHCR that it took action

---

[98] Section 255(5) of Tanzania's Criminal Procedure and Evidence Act allows the magistrate to discharge an accused person after a case has been adjourned several times (not specified) and no certificate of extension of time has been filed. Human Rights Watch interviews, magistrate, Kibondo district court, Tanzania, November 8, 1999 and UNHCR Sexual and Gender-Based Project lawyer, Kibondo, Tanzania, November 7, 1999.

[99] Statistics given to Human Rights Watch by UNHCR protection officer, Kasulu, Tanzania, November 3, 1999.

[100] In the Kasulu camps, local NGOs and UNHCR community services implementing partners (Christian Outreach, Africare, and Diocese of Western Tanganyika) maintain records of cases of rape, domestic violence, early marriage and abduction, and sexual harassment. In the Kibondo camps, the IRC, Dutch Relief Agency, and UMATI maintain records of similar cases, and in the Ngara camps, the Norwegian people's Agency maintains the same records.

[101] UNHCR document provided to Human Rights Watch by the UNHCR protection officer for Ngara, Ngara, November 11, 1999.

[102] Statistics of rape from IRC Sexual and Gender-Based Project monthly reports for 1999 given to Human Rights Watch by IRC community services officers, Kibondo Tanzania, November 6, 1999.

nevertheless to ensure that victims and witnesses received notification of the court date and were able to attend court.[103]

At this writing, it is too early to draw conclusions about the impact of UNHCR's new programs on the lives of refugee women victims of rape in the Tanzanian camps. In general, during its 1999 visits, Human Rights Watch noted a marked and welcome increase in the level of support being offered to victims of sexual violence, as well as a greater community involvement in apprehending those responsible for sexual violence in the camps.

Yet rape and other sexual violence continue to be a persistent problem in the camps. Women continue to be attacked when they leave the camps to collect firewood, as there is no fuel provision; women refugees at the Kasulu and Ngara camps complained that they sometimes had to travel more than sixty kilometers (thirty-eight miles) outside the camps to gather firewood.[104] Moreover, UNHCR's programs against sexual violence could be improved in certain key ways: they should be implemented comprehensively in all refugee camps; UNHCR staff should systematically follow-up all cases of sexual violence in the camps; and there should be clear coordination between UNHCR protection officers and community services officers in the camps to ensure that women are fully informed about their legal and other rights and are accompanied by individuals able to represent their interests during legal proceedings.

During meetings with UNHCR representatives and Tanzanian government officials in Dar-es-Salam in November 1999, Human Rights Watch expressed concern that cases of rape and sexual violence in the refugee camps were not adequately investigated and punished. In response, the UNHCR Resident Representative assured Human Rights Watch that she recognized the need for UNHCR to intensify its monitoring and follow-up of cases, and that UNHCR's program in response to violence against women, then in its initial stages, would ensure that all refugee victims of rape and other crimes would be informed about

---

[103] Assistant protection officers are local Tanzanian staff hired to carry out some of the protection duties, under the supervision of a protection officer. The assistant protection officer's duties include helping the protection office with the broad protection and security issues in the camps, including protecting refugee women, and ensuring that the perpetrators of violence against refugee women are prosecuted. Human Rights Watch interview, UNHCR protection officer, Ngara, November 11, 1999.

[104] Human Rights Watch interviews, women representatives, Mtabila 1 and 2 camps, Tanzania, November 2, 1999 and women representatives, Lukole A and B camps, Tanzania, November 11, 1999.

how to report such abuses and about the services available to victims.[105] For their part, Tanzanian government officials pointed to a lack of resources as a major stumbling block affecting their capacity to investigate and prosecute cases aggressively.[106]

Cases of Rape and other Sexual Violence

Human Rights Watch received a number of testimonies from rape victims during its visits to the Tanzanian refugee camps in May/June 1998 and October/November 1999. These illustrate the nature and extent of injuries, including psychological trauma, experienced by victims, and the shortcomings of UNHCR staff and the Tanzanian police.

Mary U. reported her rape to UNHCR and Africare, a humanitarian organization that provides community services programs, in April 1999. Mary U. is a fifteen-year-old resident in Mtabila 1 camp in Kasulu district. She was raped by two Tanzanian villagers in April 1999 while in the forest gathering firewood with a female friend. Her friend managed to escape, but Mary U. was raped by two local Tanzanians. She and her mother immediately reported the case to the police and sought medical attention from the camp clinic. However, the perpetrators had not been arrested at the time Human Rights Watch interviewed Mary U, although she could identify them, and saw one of the perpetrators again in October 1999.[107]

Agnes V., a fifteen-year-old primary student, was raped by a neighbor on April 2, 1999, as she was returning from school with several friends. The neighbor called her over and offered to pay her 10,000 Tanzania shillings (U.S.$12.50) to have sex with him. He then raped her when she refused. Agnes V.'s parents reported the case to the abashingatahe, who told the rapist to pay her father compensation. The rapist refused to do so and went to the police to accuse Agnes V.'s father of threatening him. Agnes V.'s father would not let her report the rape to the police, but she said the rapist had ruined her life and that she wanted the rapist jailed.[108]

---

[105] Human Rights Watch interview, UNHCR officers, Dar-es-Salaam, Tanzania, November 16, 1999.

[106] Human Rights Watch interview, Director of Refugees,MHA, Tanzania, November 17, 1999. *See* also the section on "Tanzania Government Response" below.

[107] Human Rights Watch interview, Mary U., Mtabila 1 camp, Tanzania, November 1, 1999. In order to decrease the tension between local villagers and the refugee community, Tanzanian villagers are given access to some refugee services, such as the use of camp clinic facilities, as in this case.

[108] Human Rights Watch interview, Agnes V., Mtabila 2 camp, November 2, 1999.

Adelina R., also sixteen years old, was raped in October 1999, while collecting firewood outside Kanembwa camp, by a refugee she described as a fifteen-year-old boy. At the same time, Adelina R.'s friend, accompanying her, was raped by another boy. Adelina R. reported the rape to police and to local village leaders, and the latter searched for the culprits and found and handed over one of them, Adelina R.'s abuser, to the Tanzanian police. However, he was released and subsequently fled. After being raped, Adelina R. was given antibiotics and injections, though she was not sure what these were for and neither UNHCR nor IRC community services officers followed up to ensure that the accused was rearrested or to provide Adelina R. with counseling.[109]

Marie-Claire E., who fled to Tanzania with her mother, sister, and brother in 1996, after their father was killed in Burundi, was sixteen years old and living in Mtendeli camp when Human Rights Watch interviewed her. She said that she had been on her way to Kanembwa camp with her younger brother on March 30, 1998, in order to visit their uncle, when she was raped by two men who spoke *Kiha*, a local Tanzanian language. She reported the case to the police the same day, but no arrests had been made by the time that she spoke to Human Rights Watch two months later. She stated, "The two men took off my clothes, in the presence of my brother. They blindfolded and raped me, one after the other. I would like the assailants to be punished for raping me."[110]

Most refugee women Human Rights Watch interviewed in 1998 complained that the Tanzanian police were reluctant to investigate rape cases in which the alleged perpetrators were Tanzanian.[111] It was hoped, however, that this problem would be overcome by the deployment in September 1999 of a new security contingent of approximately 260 police officers to the refugee camps. UNHCR told Human Rights Watch that it planned to train the new contingent in proper policing of the camps and in handling victims of sexual and domestic violence.[112]

Esperance K., who was pregnant at the time, was the victim of a rape attempt by a Burundian refugee near Kanembwa camp in April 1998. She recognized the man as her neighbor. He threatened to stab her. Then he cut her on her fingers with

---

[109] Human Rights Watch interview, Adelina R., Kanembwa camp, Tanzania, November 6, 1999.

[110] Human Rights Watch interview, Marie-Claire E., Mtendeli camp, Tanzania, June 3, 1998.

[111] *See* section on "The Tanzanian Government Response" for details on police bias and reluctance to investigate cases of rape in which the perpetrators were Tanzanians.

[112] Human Rights Watch interview, UNHCR international security liaison officer, Kigoma, Tanzania, October 28, 1999.

a knife when she resisted him, but ran off when he heard other people approaching. Esperance K. reported the attack to refugee leaders and the police, but two months later, the assailant had still not been arrested.[113]

In another case, a fourteen-year-old boy from Muyovosi camp, who allegedly raped a three-year-old girl,[114] was released from Kasulu police station without charge, despite the intervention of UNHCR, the MHA, and the child's parents. It was not clear whether he was later arrested. In another case, a refugee who worked for the Red Cross at Mtabila extension camp raped a fourteen-year-old girl in June 1997. The rapist was not arrested even though the victim reported the assault to the police.[115]

In some cases reported to Human Rights Watch, victims of rape suffered further physical and psychological abuse at the hands of their husbands, either because they believed that their wife had somehow been to blame or because she had reported a relative to the police without her husband's permission. For example, Elizabeth B., an eighteen-year-old refugee from Mtendeli camp, said she was raped by another refugee on May 17, 1998, while she was on her way to Kanembwa camp to visit her parents. She stated, "After raping me, the man took the shoes I was wearing and the money I had and fled. When I told my husband about the rape, he blamed me for the rape and started beating me."[116]

Similarly, Margarita Q., a thirty-five-year-old woman, said she was raped by a group of young Tanzanians while fleeing from Burundi in 1996. When her husband found out, he blamed her, refused to sleep with her, and began beating her up: "My husband became more and more violent about the rape, such that I fled from him on May 20, 1998. I spent three weeks without a place to stay. I stayed with different people in the camp."[117]

Seven-year-old Nandiwe D. was raped in Kanembwa camp by her paternal uncle. Her mother reported the attack to the Tanzanian police, and the uncle was

---

[113] Human Rights Watch interview, Esperance K., Kanembwa camp, Tanzania, June 3, 1998.

[114] Human Rights Watch obtained this information from the files of a community services organization working with refugees in Muyovosi camp, Tanzania, May 26, 1998. The name of organization has been withheld at its request.

[115] Human Rights Watch interview, UNHCR assistant protection officer, Kasulu district, Tanzania, May 26, 1998.

[116] Human Rights Watch interview, Elizabeth B., Kanembwa camp, Tanzania, June 3, 1998.

[117] Human Rights Watch interview, Margarita Q., Mtendeli camp, Tanzania, June 7, 1998.

arrested, but her husband threw Nandiwe's mother out of their home for causing his brother's arrest, and refugee leaders condemned her for reporting another Burundian refugee to the Tanzanian authorities. The rapist was then released by the police at the request of the victim's father. But, according to the mother, the seven-year-old had been brutally abused:

> I left Nandiwe and her older sisters at home with Andrias, my husband's brother, with whom we stay. I expected Nandiwe and her sister to follow me where I was planting beans. Later on, the older sister came alone, and she told me that Andrias had refused to let Nandiwe come to the valley. I immediately went home to check if Nandiwe was safe. When I got home, I found Andrias having sex with her in our house. I checked the child, and her vagina was hurt and bleeding. Her vagina was so badly swollen that she could not walk properly. I took her to the hospital, and she received treatment.[118]

In a similar case, Godelieve C. feared that her husband would assault her if she tried to press charges against a refugee neighbor in his twenties who had raped her ten-year-old daughter and sexually abused her two sisters. As a result, the ten-year-old contracted a vaginal infection, and the case was brought to UNHCR's attention. The family of the rapist then offered to pay the girl's family if they dropped the charges. When the girl's family agreed, the accused was released after some time in police custody. The mother told Human Rights Watch:

> I wanted to follow the law and get justice for my child, but the neighbor offered money instead, and my husband accepted the money. I wanted to insist that we take the case to court for my daughter, but I feared my husband would beat me if I kept pushing. I am angry for what has happened, but by the grace of God, my little girl did not get a fatal disease. This kind of thing happens all the time in the camp.[119]

Some rape cases have been investigated and successfully prosecuted in court. Thus, one refugee in Nduta camp, was prosecuted and imprisoned for raping three

---

[118] Human Rights Watch interview, Maria U., Kanembwa camp, Tanzania, June 3, 1998.
[119] Human Rights Watch interview, Godelieve C., Muyovosi camp, Tanzania, May 28, 1998.

young children in September 1999. The mother of one of the victims told Human Rights Watch:

> Clemence always used to play with Minauri outside our house, so when he called the child to his house on September 17, 1999, I did not suspect anything bad would happen. However, when it started to get dark before Minauri came back home, I followed her to Clemence's house. When I asked Clemence about Minauri, he denied that she was in his house, when in fact she was sleeping in his bed. I left and went back home. At about 8:00 p.m., Minauri came home in the darkness by herself. When I asked her where she was, she started crying saying that she was with Clemence, and he had forced her to have sex with him. Minauri complained about pains in her vagina. I took Minauri to Nduta camp clinic, and the doctor confirmed that she had been raped. The doctor treated the child, and I took her back home. I reported the case to the police the following day, and the police told me they were actually looking for Clemence for another case of rape of a child. In November 1999, the police told me that Clemence was arrested and is in jail.[120]

---

[120] Human Rights Watch interview, Sibisoniya N., Nduta camp, Tanzania, November 8, 1999.

VI. INTERNATIONAL HUMAN RIGHTS AND TANZANIAN LAW

International human rights law requires governments to provide protection against violence to all persons within their territory, to investigate and punish perpetrators of violence, and to ensure equal access and protection under the law to all without discrimination on the basis of race, color, sex, national origin, or other grounds.[121] These obligations extend to all refugees and asylum seekers within a host country, and the duty to protect such individuals is a primary responsibility of that host country.[122] Since the basic rights of refugees are no longer protected by the governments of their home countries, the international community also assumes the responsibility of ensuring that the rights of refugees are respected,[123] and the office of the UNHCR has been mandated to provide such international protection to refugees and works with host governments in pursuit of this objective.[124]

Many governments have been slow to respond to violence against women when perpetrated by private individuals, regardless of whether the individuals are nationals of the country, visitors, or refugees. Nonetheless, states have an affirmative obligation to "exercise due diligence to prevent, investigate, and, in accordance with national legislation, punish acts of violence against women,

---

[121] Article 2(1) of the International Covenant on Civil and Political Rights (ICCPR) states, "Each State Party to the Covenant undertakes to respect and to ensure to all individuals within its territory and subject to its jurisdiction the rights recognized in the present Covenant, without distinction of any kind, such as race, color, sex, language, religion, political or other opinion, national or social origin, property, birth or other status." Article 26 further provides that all persons are "equal before the law and are entitled without discrimination to the equal protection of the law." Tanzania ratified the ICCPR in 1983.

[122] Report of the U.N. High Commissioner for Refugees, 38 U.N. GAOR Supp. (no.12) p. 8, U.N. Doc. A/38/12(1983).

[123] Article 35 of the 1951 U.N. Convention Relating to the Status of Refugees provides, "The Contracting States undertake to cooperate with the office of the United Nations High Commissioner for Refugees, or any other agency of the United Nations which may succeed it, in the exercise of its functions, and shall in particular facilitate its duty of supervising the application of the provisions of this Convention."

[124] Chapter 1(1) of the 1950 Statute of the Office of the High Commissioner for Refugees provides, "The United Nations High Commissioner for Refugees, acting under the authority of the General Assembly, shall assume the function of providing international protection, under the auspices of the United Nations, to refugees who fall within the scope of the present statute and of seeking permanent solutions for the problem of refugees by assisting governments."

51

whether those acts are perpetrated by the states or by private persons."[125] Thus, the Tanzanian government has an affirmative obligation to protect women refugees from sexual and domestic violence and to ensure that women who are subjected to these assaults have full access to the Tanzanian legal system. By failing to ensure that police and court officials investigate, prosecute, and punish perpetrators of domestic and sexual violence against refugee women, Tanzania fails to comply with its international law obligations to provide women equal protection of the law as described below.

The 1951 U.N. Convention Relating to the Status of Refugees (Refugee Convention)[126] requires host governments to apply their national laws and make their national courts and legal assistance equally available to refugees.[127] Tanzania ratified the Refugee Convention in 1983 and thus must ensure that its national laws and courts are accessible to refugees in Tanzania who are in need of pursuing legal redress through the courts. Tanzania ratified the Convention on the Elimination of All Forms of Discrimination against Women (CEDAW) in 1985. This convention details states' obligations to ensure non-discrimination on the basis of gender and to ensure equal access to the law for all women in its territory, including refugee women.[128] When the government of Tanzania does not prohibit, or routinely fails to respond to, sexual and domestic violence against refugee women within its territory, it sends the message that such attacks will be tolerated without punishment. In doing so, Tanzania fails to exercise due diligence to protect refugee women's rights to physical integrity and, in extreme cases, to life.

In international human rights law there is increasing recognition of a woman's right to sexual autonomy, including her right to be free from nonconsensual sexual relations, including within marriage, and her right to engage in consensual sexual

---

[125] U.N. General Assembly, *Declaration on the Elimination of Violence against Women,* U.N. General Assembly Resolution 48/104 (A/RES/48/104) Art.4 (c).

[126] The 1951 U.N. Convention Relating to the Status of Refugees provides the internationally recognized general definition of the term "refugee," and details refugees' rights. States parties to the Convention are legally required to enforce its provisions to protect refugees' rights within their territories.

[127] Article 16(2) of the 1951 Convention Relating to the Status of Refugees states, "A refugee shall enjoy in the Contracting State in which he has his habitual residence the same treatment as a national in matters pertaining to access to the courts, including legal assistance."

[128] Once a state ratifies CEDAW, it becomes legally bound to enforce the provisions of CEDAW to eradicate all forms of gender-based discrimination against women in its territory.

relations. At the U.N. International Conference on Population and Development held in October 1994 in Cairo, Egypt, and the U.N. Fourth World Conference on Women held in September 1995 in Beijing, China, governments explicitly endorsed women's reproductive and sexual autonomy.[129] In the 1994 Cairo Programme of Action on Population and Development, delegates from governments around the world pledged to "eliminate all practices that discriminate against women; assist women to establish and realize their rights, including those that relate to reproductive and sexual health."[130] In the 1995 Beijing Declaration and Platform for Action,[131] delegates from governments around the world recognized that "human rights of women include their right to have control over and decide freely and responsibly on matters related to their sexuality, free of coercion, discrimination and violence."[132] Sexual autonomy is closely linked to the rights to physical security and bodily integrity, the right to consent to and freely enter into a marriage, as well as equal rights within the marriage.[133] When women are subjected to sexual coercion, be it outside a marriage or within, with no possibility for redress, a woman's right to make free decisions regarding her sexual relations is violated. Lack of sexual autonomy may also expose women to serious risks to their reproductive and sexual health. Victims of rape may face reproductive health problems, including sexually transmitted diseases such as HIV/AIDS, unwanted

---

[129] The United Nations International Conference on Population and Development (ICPD), held in Cairo, Egypt, in October 1994, focused on promoting gender equality and equity. The conference concluded by adopting a program of action, United Nations, *Gender Equality, Equity and Empowerment of Women* (New York: United Nations Publications, 1994), A/CONF.171/13, 18 October, 1994, whereby countries pledged to promote the full participation and partnership of women and men in productive and reproductive life. The United Nations Fourth World Conference on Women, held in Beijing, China, in October 1995, focused on strategic actions for promoting women's human rights.

[130] United Nations, *Cairo Programme of Action on Population and Development*, paragraph 4.4(c).

[131] United Nations, *Beijing Declaration and Platform for Action* (New York: United Nations Publications, 1995), A/CONF.177/20, 17 October 1995, adopted at the Fourth World Conference on Women held in Beijing, China, in September 1995. This document was adopted by over 200 countries participating in the conference by consensus and is meant to reaffirm the commitment of all states to fulfill their obligation to promote universal respect for, and observance and protection of, all rights of women throughout their life cycle, including women's reproductive rights.

[132] United Nations, *Beijing Declaration and Platform for Action*, paragraph 223.

[133] Article 23 of the ICCPR. *See also* Article 16 of the Universal Declaration of Human Rights.

pregnancy, miscarriages, complications resulting from unsafe abortions and other gynecological injuries, maternal mortality, psychological trauma, and social stigmatization.

In theory, Tanzanian law provides female victims of violence with some protection and recourse when they are raped or otherwise physically assaulted. In 1998, Tanzania passed the Sexual Offences Special Provisions Act, which adopted more targeted penalties for crimes including rape, attempted rape, and statutory rape. Under the act, rape is punishable by up to thirty years of imprisonment and attempted rape is punishable by a prison sentence of up to ten years.[134] Statutory rape, defined as sex with a girl under fifteen years old, is punishable by a death sentence or life imprisonment.[135] Tanzania has not yet enacted explicit legislation that criminalizes domestic violence, but physical assault within a domestic setting should be punishable under the common law of assault in Tanzania.

Refugee women in Tanzania have been largely unable to obtain the legal redress to which they are entitled, particularly in cases of domestic violence. Since the beginning of 1999, there has been an increase in efforts by UNHCR to mobilize Tanzanian officials, including police, to assist refugee women victims of rape in accessing justice through the Tanzanian courts. Unfortunately, this has not been the case with regard to domestic violence.[136] Women victims of domestic violence face significant obstacles in mobilizing the law to protect them. There is overwhelming resistance among Tanzanian officials, including the police, to prosecuting cases of domestic violence, as discussed below. Further, women refugees are reluctant to turn to the Tanzanian justice system as a means of resolving domestic violence cases for a variety of reasons—because they lack confidence in the police, because they fear being ostracized by other refugees if they report their compatriots, and for fear that their husbands or partners, on whom they may be dependent, or to whom they retain and emotional attachment, may be jailed. In short, the current system provides them little or no recourse or remedy against domestic violence.

---

[134] Sections 6, 3, and 8 of the Sexual Offences Special Provisions Act, 1998. These provisions amended the Tanzanian Criminal Penal Code, which carried life imprisonment as punishment for rape. Human Rights Watch opposes the death penalty in relation to any crime, including crimes of sexual violence, because it is inherently cruel and often subject to discriminatory application.

[135] Ibid., section 11.

[136] The section on "The Response of UNHCR" has details on the positive and negative aspects of community- based mechanisms and courts of law, as institutions often relied upon when responding to domestic violence.

VII. TANZANIAN GOVERNMENT RESPONSE

Tanzania generously provided refuge to hundreds of thousands of refugees from other African countries over many years, in some cases offering them land for settlement, integration, and citizenship. Currently the country hosts over 600,000[137] refugees, the majority of whom fled conflicts in Burundi, the Democratic Republic of Congo, and Rwanda. Ethnic Hutu Burundians constitute the majority of this refugee population. This continuing influx of refugees has sparked a degree of xenophobia and growing hostility among Tanzanians, who point to the serious security, financial, and environmental impact that large refugee influxes have on their country. At times, the Tanzanian government has reacted to such influxes by violating international refugee law.[138] For the most part however, Tanzania continues to accept refugees, provide them with asylum, and coordinate with UNHCR to set up mechanisms that afford refugees greater assistance and protection.

In meetings with Human Rights Watch, Tanzanian government officials in Dar-es-Salaam expressed concern about the exposure of refugee women to sexual and domestic violence, but said they lacked the necessary resources to ensure law enforcement and to provide adequate judicial services in the areas in which the refugee camps are located.[139] In visiting the camps, it was clear to Human Rights Watch that Tanzanian police and judicial authorities are certainly hampered by a lack of personnel and a shortage of material resources, though there were also problems arising from bias on the part of local police, camp commanders, and magistrates regarding violence against women, and against refugees generally. Indeed, refugees repeatedly complained that police refused to take seriously or investigate their complaints, particularly when the alleged assailant was a Tanzanian.

---

[137] UNHCR figures as of March 2000.

[138] Fearing the militarization of its borders and arguing that it had to protect Tanzanian citizens living close to the borders with Burundi and Rwanda, in late 1997 the Tanzanian government began forced round-ups of foreigners living in those areas and confined them to refugee camps in western Tanzania. For a detailed analysis of this issue, see Human Rights Watch, "In the Name of Security: Forced Round-Ups of Refugees in Tanzania," *A Human Rights Watch Short Report*, vol. 11, no. 4, July 1999.

[139] Human Rights Watch interviews,MHA officials, Bernard Mchomvu, MHA principal secretary; Caroline Mchome, Refugee Department legal protection head; Johnson Brahim, Refugee Department project head; and Patrick Tsere, principal refugee officer, Dar-es-Salaam, Tanzania, June 10, 1998.

While noting significant improvements in other respects between its 1998 and 1999 visits to the camps, Human Rights Watch could not discern any significant changes either in police and related resources or in attitudes. Acute lack of resources available to local police and courts persists and hinders the police and courts from functioning effectively. The district courts in the Kigoma area were understaffed; the Kasulu and Kibondo districts each had only one district magistrate: they have to deal with all criminal cases from the refugee camps, as well as the wider Tanzanian community. Minor improvements had been made thanks to the provision of funding, stationery, and radios, to the magistrate and police by UNHCR in 1999.

The MHA's Refugee Department, in Dar-es-Salaam, is responsible for overseeing all matters concerning refugees, including camp administration, security, and ensuring the application of Tanzanian laws to refugees and relief agencies operating in the camps. The Refugee Department has deployed one officer, known as the camp commander, to each refugee camp. This officer oversees the camp's administration and security at the field level and monitor the movement of refugees, including issuing passes to travel outside the camps.[140] The MHA has also deployed at least twenty police officers to each of the Burundian camps visited by Human Rights Watch in order to maintain law and order in the camps. These police were deployed in 1998 under a security agreement funded by UNHCR. Camp commanders, police, and UNHCR officials all work closely together to address the administrative and security needs of refugees in the camps.

The Camp Commanders

In each camp, the commanders have established refugee administrative structures to improve camp security. These structures are composed of four groups of refugees who report cases of violence in the camps to camp commanders: young

---

[140] The camp commander position is purely administrative and the person has no authority to investigate crimes occurring in the camps. Rather, the camp commanders coordinate with the police to ensure security within the camps. In cases in which the camp commanders receive complaints of a criminal nature from the refugees, they are supposed to refer such complaints to the police for investigation.

male refugees (known as *sungu-sungus*),[141] who patrol the camps and report violent incidents and other disputes to block leaders;[142] women's representatives, who receive complaints from women refugees, including cases of domestic and sexual violence, and report these to block leaders; block leaders themselves who receive and pass on all complaints to UNHCR, the Tanzanian authorities, or the abashingatahe; and the abashingatahe, who preside over certain cases and refer others to the camp commander and UNHCR officers.[143]

Most camp commanders Human Rights Watch interviewed in 1998 expressed concern about the security of Burundian refugee women, but this rarely seemed to translate into a serious effort to combat violence.[144] Some camp commanders did not consider domestic violence to be a crime to be punished in the courts and were reluctant to refer allegations to police for investigation. Rather, they sought to reconcile the parties. This approach may have been successful in some cases, but in others put women at greater physical risk. The commander of Mtendeli camp, for example, told Human Rights Watch that it was better to counsel the parties in order to resolve domestic violence, rather than refer the abuser for prosecution. "Even in Tanzania, a man does not get arrested for beating his wife."[145] At Kanembwa camp, the commander said refugee women depended on their husbands, and so, in domestic disputes, it was "best to reconcile them."[146] Similarly in Mtabila camp, the commander, a woman, said her approach was to "pacify or reconcile,"

---

[141] Generally within Tanzania, the sungu sungu are neighborhood civil defense forces organized at the village level to assist the police to combat crime. They are selected by the community and represent them at local government meetings. They receive no formal training from the police or army and are not officially armed. A similar structure has been set up within the refugee camps, relying on male refugees to augment security within the camps.

[142] Most refugee camps are divided into small units or "blocks" in a village-like style to facilitate UNHCR's management of the camps. Each block can hold more than five hundred refugees, depending on the size of the camp. In Tanzania, most camps were divided into four blocks. UNHCR had no formal statistics on the number of refugees per block.

[143] *See* the section below on "The Response of UNHCR," where details on the abashingatahe's criteria for choosing cases to be dealt with by the village council and those that are referred to UNHCR and camp commanders are discussed.

[144] Human Rights Watch interviewed the camp commanders for the following four camps: Kanembwa, Mtabila, Mtendeli, and Nduta, in May and June 1998.

[145] Human Rights Watch interview, camp commander, Mtendeli camp, Tanzania, June 8, 1998.

[146] Human Rights Watch interview, camp commander, Kanembwa camp, Tanzania, June 3, 1998.

though she acknowledged the need to arrest and punish perpetrators. She stated: "Women are reluctant to come forward. We need to do more work to create an environment in which victims of domestic violence can feel safe enough to report cases to the police."[147] Camp commanders were more prepared to condemn sexual violence than domestic violence, and they normally referred rape allegations to police for investigation.

Police

Tanzanian police deployed to the refugee camps are responsible for maintaining law and order and preventing and investigating crime, including allegations of assault and rape. Human Rights Watch is concerned, however, that police did not take adequate measures either to prevent, or to respond to, violence against women refugees, and are affected by bias, a degree of corruption, a general lack of awareness about the seriousness of such abuses, and a lack of resources. Police attitudes toward domestic violence were disturbing and it was evident that many police officers did not really consider domestic violence a crime. In Kibondo, for example, rather than investigate reports of domestic violence, the police simply refer the victims to UNHCR and other organizations for counseling.[148]

Some Burundian refugee women interviewed by Human Rights Watch complained that police were biased against complainants when the person accused was a Tanzanian national.[149] Some police officers, however, told Human Rights Watch that no Tanzanians had been responsible for rapes of refugee women, but that was contradicted by other sources, including women who said they had been raped.[150] One police officer insisted to Human Rights Watch that "refugees were

---

[147] Human Rights Watch interview, camp commander, Mtabila camp, Tanzania, May 28, 1998.

[148] When we asked the police in the Kibondo camps why they did not investigate cases of domestic violence, a typical response was, "Domestic violence is dealt with by staff of the IRC Sexual and Gender-Based Violence Project." The IRC Sexual and Gender-Based Violence Project is a counseling and community education awareness project for refugees. The project is based in the Kibondo camps.

[149] Human Rights Watch interview, group interview with Burundian women refugees in Mtendeli and Nduta camps, Tanzania, June 6 and June 7, 1998.

[150] Human Rights Watch interview, police officers, police post, Mtendeli camp, Tanzania, June 8, 1998.

being raped by other refugees, not by Tanzanians."[151] But some women whom we interviewed in May and June 1998 clearly alleged that they had been raped by local Tanzanians, and two months later no arrests had been made.[152] Police told Human Rights Watch that they had no record of the case.[153]

Other women told Human Rights Watch that police refused to investigate complaints unless they were first paid a bribe. Soplange S., for example, whose case is reported above, said that police warned her husband to stop beating her only after she had paid them 4,000 Tanzanian shillings (U.S.$7.00), and then refused to take action when she went to them again but was unable to pay more money. She stated: "The police need money. They do not come to your rescue for nothing. When they ask for money, they use the word *chai* [the word for "tea" in Kiswahili] referring to money for a bribe."[154] According to Annette G., whose case is also reported earlier, the police were not willing to help her:

> I no longer bother to report the case to the police because they failed to assist me on previous occasions when my husband beat me. When I reported the case to the police at Kanembwa camp, they did not follow up on my report. My husband started beating me worse, knowing that he would not be arrested for beating me.[155]

Further, in Nduta camp, Virginie M. said the police would not arrest her husband, though he assaulted her many times, because he was friendly with a senior police officer:

> Whenever I report my husband to the police for beating me, they do nothing to respond to my complaint. On several occasions I have gone to the Nduta camp police post to report the same case, but the police still

---

[151] Human Rights Watch interview, police official, Kibondo district, Tanzania, June 9, 1998.

[152] Human Rights Watch interview, Marie-Claire E., Mtendeli camp, Tanzania, June 9, 1998.

[153] Human Rights Watch interview, police officer, Mtendeli camp, Tanzania, June 9, 1998.

[154] Human Rights Watch interview, Soplange S., Kanembwa camp, Tanzania, June 3, 1998.

[155] Human Rights Watch interview, Annette G., Kanembwa camp, Tanzania, June 3, 1998.

leave my husband free to continue beating me, because my husband is a friend of the senior police officer.[156]

The deployment of approximately 250 more police in September 1999, it was hoped, would bring about improvements.[157] However, the officers, each of whom was to spend six months in the camps, received no special training before their deployment on how to protect women refugees from sexual and domestic violence. UNHCR's international security liaison officer said that training on policing refugee camps was planned, but some of the police officers interviewed by Human Rights Watch in November 1999 appeared to consider domestic violence of little relevance to them, and explained how they counseled victims to return to their husbands. One said she had advised a victim: "Your husband will be jailed. How will you raise the children by yourself, and how will you explain this to your in-laws in Burundi?"[158] In another meeting, seven women police officers told Human Rights Watch that "domestic violence is not an offence in Tanzania,"[159] indicating a need for them to be trained on how properly to respond to and address the problem. By contrast, police readily accepted the need to investigate rape cases in the camps.[160]

The Courts
Discriminatory attitudes and a shortage of personnel with expertise to handle violent crimes against women, as well as other resource problems, prevent the Tanzanian courts from responding adequately to domestic and sexual violence. In June 1998, the district court in Kibondo, to which the cases from the Mtendeli, Kanembwa, Nduta, and Mkugwa camps are referred, was being run by two male

---

[156] Human Rights Watch interview, Virginie M., Nduta camp, Tanzania, June 6, 1998.

[157] Human Rights Watch interview, UNHCR international security liaison officer, Kigoma, Tanzania, October 28, 1999.

[158] Human Rights Watch interview, police officer, Nduta camp, Tanzania, November 8, 1999.

[159] Human Rights Watch interview, police officers, Ngara camps, Tanzania, November 11, 1999.

[160] Human Rights Watch interview, police officers, Kibondo and Ngara camps, Tanzania, October and November 1999. The senior police officer in Kasulu district was not available to be interviewed or to give us permission to interview police officers deployed to the Kasulu camps. As a result, we did not conduct police interviews in the Kasulu camps.

police prosecutors,[161] a male magistrate, and a male court interpreter. None had been trained to investigate or prosecute domestic or sexual assault cases, and no female staff were available to record evidence from women victims. The magistrate, in fact, said that the two police prosecutors had not been trained to prosecute any crimes,[162] and that poor investigations and inept prosecutions frequently resulted in the acquittal of defendants charged with raping refugee women.[163]

Despite his critique of the inadequate investigation and prosecution of sex crimes against refugee women, this magistrate expressed no wish to have domestic violence cases result in criminal prosecutions. On the contrary, he said, he referred all such cases for out-of-court settlement. He stated: "Only four domestic violence cases have so far been brought to the court. However, I referred them to the camps to be dealt with by UNHCR officers and other NGOs through counseling."[164]

It is not only the lack of awareness and resources or the attitudes of magistrates, police, and prosecutors that stand in the way of prosecutions, it is also women refugees' own reluctance to bring cases before the courts. The Ngara magistrate told Human Rights Watch that women victims of domestic violence did not wish their husbands to be incarcerated,[165] so they often made complaints but then "withdrew" them after "reconciling" with their abusers. He commented: "If a person does not want to come forward, you cannot force her," and said that when police did try to bring cases to court, women would say, 'We have reconciled,' leaving the police simply to warn the men not to assault her again.[166]

A similar picture emerged from the Kibondo, Kasulu, Ngara, and Kigoma courts, with the Kibondo magistrate complaining about the acute lack of the most basic materials, including paper to write on and to use for maintaining case

----

[161] Police prosecutors are trained police officers who are upgraded to prosecute cases in court.

[162] Human Rights Watch interview, magistrate, Kibondo district court, Tanzania, June 9, 1998.

[163] Ibid.

[164] Ibid.

[165] Human Rights Watch interview, magistrate, Ngara district court, Tanzania, November 11, 1999.

[166] Human Rights Watch interview, public prosecutor, Ngara district court, Tanzania, November 11, 1999.

records.[167] A High Court judge told Human Rights Watch that it was difficult to attract trained lawyers and prosecutors to work in these areas due to their remoteness, so further undermining the administration of justice there.[168]

Conditions had scarcely improved when Human Rights Watch visited again in 1999: understaffing, poor material resources, and no female staff to take reports from female victims remained problems,[169] and there were no training programs for court officials on how to deal with cases of violence against women refugees. UNHCR, however, had provided some funding for basic resources, such as stationery for the courts, and had provided the police with a car to help in bringing witnesses and suspects to court, and radios to assist communication by magistrates and police.[170]

Much international support is required for Tanzania's law enforcement and judicial systems to provide protection, remedies, and redress to women refugees or other victims of sexual or domestic abuse. In addition, there is a critical need for police and law enforcement officials to be trained in refugee and human rights law, and for programs designed to prevent violence against women.

---

[167] Human Rights Watch interview, magistrate, Kibondo district court, Tanzania, June 9, 1998.

[168] Human Rights Watch interview, judge of the High Court of Tanzania, Kigoma, May 26, 1998.

[169] Human Rights Watch interviews, magistrate, Kasulu district court, Tanzania, November 2, 1999 and magistrate, Kibondo district court, November 8, 1999.

[170] Ibid.

VIII. THE RESPONSE OF UNHCR

The extreme conditions under which refugees are often forced to flee; the consequent breakdown of family and societal structures; the location, size, design, and layout of refugee camps; women's subordinate status within their own societies; and inadequate prosecution of domestic and sexual violence in countries of origin as well as countries of refuge, are all factors that contribute to high rates of sexual and domestic violence in refugee settings. Recognizing these facts, UNHCR has issued two important sets of guidelines to direct its staff on ways to better protect women refugees. Yet, in many places around the world, UNHCR's *Guidelines on Refugee Women* have remained merely aspirational, with little or no effort made by UNHCR staff to implement these guidelines as a routine and integral part of all UNHCR programs beginning from the emergency stage of a refugee crisis.[171] In many places refugee women have been left for long periods with little or no attention paid to their protection needs, even in situations such as that in Tanzania, where UNHCR and the Tanzanian government were long ago informed of the nature and extent of the violence to which refugee women are subject.

In 1999, some five years after the establishment of the refugee camps in Tanzania, UNHCR began to address violence against women by implementing new programs and strengthening existing ones for refugee women. These efforts were undertaken partly as a result of advocacy on this issue by human rights groups and partly due to UNHCR's receipt of U.N. Foundation funds[172] in October 1998 to

---

[171] Human Rights Watch interview, Jane Lowicki, senior coordinator, Women's Commission for Refugee Women and Children, April 10, 2000. Also *see*, Women's Commission on Refugee Women and Children, *Women Displaced in the Southern Caucasus: An Examination of Humanitarian Assistance Needs in Azerbaijan, Armenia, Nagorno-Karabakh and Georgia* (New York: Women's Commission for Refugee Women and Children, April 1998).

[172] In 1997, businessman and philanthropist Ted Turner donated U.S.$1 billion to the United Nations, whereby the United Nations Foundation (U.N. Foundation) was established. The mission of the U.N. Foundation is to support the objectives of the U.N. and its Charter. The mission statement of the U.N. Foundation concerning women reads, "The U.N. Foundation will assist the United Nations in efforts to both reduce rapid population growth and encourage development through providing the information, services and opportunities that individuals and couples need to determine freely the number, spacing and timing of their children. The U.N. Foundation will support U.N. follow-up and implementation of the action plans developed at the International Conference on Population and Development and the Fourth World Conference of Women. Within this framework, the Foundation will place special emphasis on the development needs of adolescent girls and the

support programs to fight violence against refugee women in several sub-Saharan African countries. Many of these programs and efforts are commendable in their objectives, yet further action in several critical areas is needed to enable these programs to offer refugee women the greatest amount of protection. UNHCR's efforts currently to prevent and respond to violence against women in Tanzanian refugee camps are undermined in several key ways. With regard to domestic violence:

• domestic and sexual violence are treated differently, with the result that assaults, including marital rape, occurring in homes are treated with less seriousness than they warrant;
• the lack of a protocol to guide staff and refugees who deal with domestic violence victims results in haphazard handling of such cases;
• the absence of effective mechanisms to punish perpetrators of domestic violence inevitably helps to perpetuate the violence;
• the abashingatahe do not operate in accordance with international human rights norms relevant to protecting women from, and responding to, domestic violence: there are no guidelines for how they should handle such cases. No consistent efforts are made to refer cases of violence for criminal investigation or to monitor the outcome in such cases; and
• the programs overlook the role that women's fundamental inequality plays in making women vulnerable to violence.

UNHCR acknowledges the need to revise its policy on refugee women to include guidelines on domestic violence. The main issues, therefore, are when UNHCR actually adopts a policy on domestic violence, what will be the content of this policy, and how will it be enforced.

UNHCR also needs to remedy shortcomings in its response to sexual violence. Currently, these efforts lack:

• standardized implementation throughout all refugee camps;
• systematic follow-up on cases of sexual violence in the camps; and
• coordination between community services officers and protection officers to ensure that women understand their legal rights and other options and are accompanied and assisted during legal proceedings.

---

quality of reproductive health." In February 1999, the U.N. Foundation gave UNHCR the first installment of a US$1.65 million award to strengthen UNHCR's efforts to prevent sexual violence against women and adolescent girls in refugee situations in five countries in Sub-Saharan Africa: Tanzania, Kenya, Liberia, Sierra Leone, and Guinea.

UNHCR's Guidelines and their Limitations

In July 1991, UNHCR issued the *Guidelines on the Protection of Refugee Women* (hereafter *Guidelines on Refugee Women*) to assist staff in identifying and responding to the issues, problems, and risks facing refugee women.[173] Almost four years later, UNHCR issued *Sexual Violence Guidelines* to improve or initiate services to address the special needs and concerns of refugees who are at risk of or have suffered sexual violence.[174]

The *Guidelines on Refugee Women* set out measures that should be taken by UNHCR and host governments to prevent and respond to physical and sexual attacks against women during flight and in host countries. These guidelines call, among other things, for:

- changing the physical design and location of refugee camps to provide greater physical security;
- using security patrols;
- reducing the use of closed facilities or detention centers;
- training staff on the particular problems faced by refugee women and employing female staff to identify their concerns;
- educating refugee women about their rights;
- giving priority to assessing the protection needs of unaccompanied refugee women; and
- ensuring women's direct access to food and other services, including access to whatever registration process is used to determine eligibility for assistance.

In cases of rape, the *Guidelines on Refugee Women* provide that "the aim of UNHCR activities should be to ensure that the individual woman obtains protection in the future, that adequate actions are taken to prevent similar cases from occurring, that her medical and other needs resulting from the protection problem are met, and that actions are taken to institute legal proceedings if sufficient evidence can be obtained."[175] The *Guidelines on Refugee Women* also oblige UNHCR staff to take steps to redress the problem when an individual refugee

---

[173] UNHCR, *Guidelines on the Protection of Refugee Women* (Geneva: UNHCR, July 1991).

[174] UNHCR, *Sexual Violence against Refugees: Guidelines on Prevention and Response* (Geneva: UNHCR, March 1995).

[175] UNHCR, *Guidelines on Refugee Women*, p. 27.

woman's rights are violated or where a pattern of discrimination against refugee women is uncovered.

The *Sexual Violence Guidelines* supplement the *Guidelines on Refugee Women* by suggesting a range of preventive measures that can and should be taken to prevent sexual violence. These steps include:

- ensuring that the physical design and location of refugee camps enhance the physical security of women;
- providing frequent security patrols by law enforcement authorities and by the refugees themselves;
- installing fencing around the camps;
- identifying and promoting alternatives to refugee camps where possible;
- organizing inter-agency meetings among UNHCR, other relief organizations, and relevant government officials, as well as with refugees themselves, in order to develop a plan of action to prevent sexual violence; and
- assigning a greater number of female protection officers, field interpreters, doctors, health workers, and counselors to the camps.

Moreover, the *Sexual Violence Guidelines* stress that UNHCR staff have an important role to play in taking preventive measures and involving the host government in implementing those measures. In particular, UNHCR staff should stress to government authorities their duties to investigate, prosecute, and punish perpetrators of sexual violence and urge states "to adopt a firm and highly visible policy against all forms of sexual violence including that committed by government employees."[176]

The U.N. High Commissioner for Refugees' programs are supervised and approved by the UNHCR Executive Committee, which is made up of fifty-three member states. The Executive Committee has issued a number of "General Conclusions," or formalized statements, on the subject of refugee women. These statements provide guidance to states on existing international refugee law and set moral obligations and contribute to the development of states' practice in dealing with refugees within their territories. For example, Executive Committee Conclusion No.73 of 1993 sets standards which host governments must ensure when

---

[176] UNHCR, *Sexual Violence Guidelines*, p. 20.

dealing with refugee protection and sexual violence. [177] Tanzania became a member of UNHCR's Executive Committee in 1963 and thus is required to comply with the standards established under Executive Committee Conclusion No.73 in order to achieve maximum security for refugee women.

The *Sexual Violence Guidelines* provide UNHCR staff with clear methods of identifying sexual violence victims and steps to take in response. Three areas must be addressed in supporting the victim: protection and redress, medical needs, and psychosocial and counseling needs. Protecting the victim may involve contacting the police if the victim so decides and ensuring the physical safety of the victim by such measures as her "removal to a safe house, emergency room or immediate transfer from a camp."[178] The *Sexual Violence Guidelines* state that, where the alleged perpetrator of sexual violence is a member of the police, military, or a government official, "immediate measures" are necessary. Such measures are, again, dependent on the wishes of the victim and include bringing the incident to the attention of high-level officials, organizing identification lineups, and prosecuting the alleged perpetrator.[179]

There is a significant gap in UNHCR's policy *Guidelines on Refugee Women*: they do not substantively address the problem of domestic violence. In fact, the one reference to domestic abuse contained in the *Sexual Violence Guidelines*

---

[177] Under "Executive Committee Conclusion No.73 of 1993: Refugee Protection and Sexual Violence," the UNHCR Executive Committee urges states, "to respect and ensure the fundamental right of all individuals within their territory to personal security . . . by enforcing relevant national laws in compliance with international legal standards and by adopting concrete measures to prevent and combat sexual violence, including, (i) the development of training programmes aimed at promoting respect by law enforcement officers and members of military forces of the right of every individual . . . to security of person; (ii) implementation of effective and non-discriminatory legal remedies including the facilitation of the filing and investigation of complaints against sexual abuse, the prosecution of offenders, and timely and proportional disciplinary action in cases of abuse of power resulting in sexual violence; (iii) arrangements facilitating prompt and unhindered access to all asylum seekers, refugees and returnees for UNHCR and as appropriate other organizations approved by the governments concerned; (iv) activities aimed at promoting the rights of refugee women, including through the dissemination of the Guidelines on the Protection of Refugee Women and their implementation."

[178] Ibid., p. 34.

[179] Ibid., p. 37.

discourages UNHCR staff from becoming involved in domestic rape cases.[180] As a consequence, UNHCR staff have no guidance on their affirmative obligations or authority regarding domestic violence. The absence of a clear, informed, and consistent UNHCR policy on domestic violence has contributed to institutional silence on this issue, kept concerned staff from taking initiatives, and allowed other staff members to ignore the problem. Without a policy, no sustained and meaningful attention is paid to this problem.

Notwithstanding these shortcomings, the *Guidelines on Refugee Women* and the *Sexual Violence Guidelines* are important steps in raising the profile of refugee women throughout UNHCR's mission and ensuring that the needs of women are reflected in every stage of program planning. In particular, they draw critical attention to the widespread, but previously much ignored, problem of sexual violence.

Guidelines are not Enough: Implementation

UNHCR is revising its policies on refugee women to come up with a concrete policy that includes all issues affecting refugee women that UNHCR staff in the field need to address. As UNHCR's inconsistent implementation of its guidelines on sexual violence makes clear, the existence of guidelines is not enough: protection requires early and thorough implementation of such directives.

The research conducted by Human Rights Watch in Tanzania demonstrated the difficulties of translating guidelines into practice. The guidelines often were not consistently implemented by UNHCR staff in the field. Some staff had not even been apprized of or trained in the content of UNHCR's policies on women. The guidelines often were not readily available, and in some cases, UNHCR staff did not even know that they existed. Staff also did not understand that implementation of these guidelines on protection of refugee women was not a choice, but rather a routine and integral obligation on their part as UNHCR employees. By October/ November 1999 UNHCR's implementation of its guidelines had improved, thanks to its receipt

---

[180] Section 3.5 of the *Sexual Violence Guidelines* reads, "Extreme caution should be exercised before any intervention is made on sexual violence in domestic situations. Concerned staff should be aware of the possible difficulties that may arise following intervention. In some situations, more harm may be caused to the victim and other relatives by becoming involved than had the matter been left alone."

of a U.N. Foundation grant of U.S. $1.65 million to improve programs for refugee women in several African countries, including Tanzania.[181]

Human Rights Watch recognizes the financial and logistical challenges facing UNHCR in sustaining refugee protection programs, particularly in Africa. The cuts in UNHCR's budget, the focus of international attention on recent refugee crises in Europe, as well as "donor fatigue" with respect to African refugee crises, have served to limit resources available to refugees in most African countries.[182] While resources are a part of the problem, however, it is clear that UNHCR's slow progress in implementing its own guidelines on women across the board is not solely a matter of resources. Apathy and discriminatory attitudes among some UNHCR staff remain a stumbling block to consistent and routine implementation. As the

---

[181] The U.N Foundation money allocated to the Tanzanian camps for sexual and other gender related programs is a total amount of 195,681,000 Tanzanian shillings (approximately U.S.$243,000). This funding is budgeted under UNHCR's Tanzania project 00/AT/TAN/CM/256, as follows: health facilities and construction, 7,000,000 Tanzanian shillings(approximately U.S.$9,000); health facilities support, 18,900,000 Tanzanian shillings (approximately U.S.$24,000); individual family Support, 97,417,000 Tanzanian shillings (approximately U.S.$122,000); other community services support, 58,808,000 Tanzanian shillings (approximately U.S.$74,000); Training/Seminars, 4,000,000 Tanzanian shillings (approximately U.S.$5,000); and refugee legal representation, 33,600.000 Tanzanian shillings (approximately U.S.$42,000). An additional U.S.$7,400 was allocated to fund community services programs.

[182] Between March and June 1999, UNHCR received funds from donor countries equivalent to a weekly budget of U.S.$10 million for an estimated 800,000 Kosovar refugees. At the same time, UNHCR was able to raise only U.S.$1.3 million of an annual U.S.$8 million appeal for nearly half a million Sierra Leonean refugees in Guinea and Liberia, most of whom have fled almost unimaginable atrocities. In other words, in 1999 UNHCR spent about U.S.$.11 per refugee per day in Africa. The average of U.S.$1.23 spent per refugee per day in the Balkans was ten times the amount spent on African refugees. Kenneth Roth, Op-ed, "Kosovars Aren't the Only Refugees," *Wall Street Journal,* June 8, 1999; T. Christian Miller and Ann M. Simmons, "Refugee Camps in Africa and Europe," *Los Angeles Times,* May 22, 1999; Thomas Chibale-Mabwe, "U.N.'s U.S.$0.11 Insult to African Refugees," *Times of Zambia,* July 16, 1999; John Vidal, "Comments and Analysis: Blacks Need, but only Whites Receive: Race Appears to be Skewing the West's Approach to Aid. Look at Kosovo. Then Look at Africa," *Guardian,* August 12, 1999; and Stephanie Nolen, "Rape at the End of the World: This Is Not Kosovo, and You Have Not Seen These People on Your Television Screen. But They Have Been Here for Years and They Are in Danger," *Globe and Mail Metro,* August 28, 1998.

Tanzanian example illustrates, once the political will is there, much more can be done to create programs that better protect women.

The Response of UNHCR Tanzania to Domestic and Sexual Violence

In October and November 1999 Human Rights Watch returned to the Burundian refugee camps in Tanzania to find that UNHCR had, to its credit, initiated more systematic, careful, and effective efforts to address the problems of sexual and domestic violence. In 1999 UNHCR began to strengthen existing mechanisms to prevent violence against refugee women by, among other things, increasing education and awareness campaigns against gender-based violence among refugees, mobilizing refugees to engage in community-based interventions to prevent violence against women, providing counseling to victims of sexual and domestic violence, and providing legal assistance to victims of rape who wish to pursue their cases in court. These positive measures by UNHCR are a reflection of the seriousness with which UNHCR officers in Tanzania now take protection of refugee women as part of their duties. While UNHCR's current programs to protect women refugees in the Tanzanian camps are in their initial stages and will take some time to affect the lives of refugee women, they are all steps in the right direction and, once improved, should be adapted and replicated in other UNHCR programs elsewhere.

UNHCR's efforts to prevent and respond to violence against women in Tanzanian refugee camps can be further strengthened in several key ways. First, although UNHCR has expressed concern about both sexual and domestic violence, its response nonetheless has been targeted more at sexual violence. One result of this differential treatment is that domestic violence is treated as a lesser priority, which reinforces the common perception that it does not warrant an equally serious response. Second, all UNHCR programs on violence against women need to be more consistently implemented across camps. In particular, UNHCR should exercise greater oversight regarding the collection of uniform, consistent, disaggregated data on the rates of sexual and domestic violence in the various camps. Third, UNHCR follow-up on both domestic and sexual violence cases needs to be improved and standardized. Fourth, UNHCR should facilitate better coordination between community services officers and protection officers to ensure that women understand their legal rights and other options in instances of domestic or sexual violence and that women are accompanied and assisted during legal proceedings. Finally, UNHCR needs to monitor more effectively refugee-run dispute mechanisms, such as the abashingatahe, to which women go for resolution of crimes of violence, to ensure that all allegations of violence are referred for criminal investigation, and it should provide training to these community-based groups on how to handle domestic violence cases.

Since 1997, human rights and humanitarian organizations have confirmed the need for greater attention to the issue of violence against women in the Tanzanian refugee camps. In addition to Human Rights Watch, other organizations have found high rates of violence against women. The IRC concluded in 1997 that approximately 26 percent of the 3,803 Burundian refugee women they interviewed had experienced sexual violence during their flight from Burundi or while living in Kanembwa camp.[183] The Women's Commission for Refugee Women and Children (hereafter "Women's Commission"), a U.S.-based nongovernmental advocacy group, found UNHCR staff to be biased against women and dismissive of attacks against women during their visit to the Tanzanian camps to investigate the human rights conditions of Burundian refugee children and adolescents in February 1998.[184] In March 1999, Refugees International, a U.S.-based nongovernmental advocacy group, found that rape and domestic violence were rampant in the Tanzanian camps.[185]

The Situation in 1998

During its first visit to Tanzanian camps in May and June 1998, Human Rights Watch found several persistent problems, including serious understaffing of UNHCR's field offices, poor training of UNHCR staff, biased and dismissive attitudes among UNHCR staff, and a lack of resources, all of which affected how UNHCR Tanzania was administering its programs to prevent and respond to domestic and sexual violence. Human Rights Watch found too that some UNHCR staff in Tanzania tended to hide their inaction behind "cultural" excuses when asked about cases of violence against refugee women in Tanzanian camps. For example, one UNHCR field office head acknowledged that domestic violence was occurring in the camps but described the level of violence as "not disturbing" and as the "normal

[183] IRC, *Pain Too Deep for Tears*, p. 3.

[184] The Women's Commission on Refugee Women and Children, *A Child's Nightmare: Burundian Children at Risk* (New York: Women's Commission on Refugee Women and Children, May 1998).

[185] Refugees International, *Hope in the Fight to Reduce Gender Violence in Tanzanian Refugee Camps* (Washington, DC: Refugees International, May 26, 1999).

amount."[186]   Another UNHCR protection officer attributed sexual and domestic violence to Burundian culture.[187]

Some UNHCR staff interviewed by Human Rights Watch in 1998 simply did not recognize protecting women refugees from sexual and domestic violence to be part of their protection duties. UNHCR protection staff in all of the camps visited maintained some record of cases of sexual and domestic violence against refugee women, but there were neither proactive, preventive strategies nor regular follow-up to ensure that cases were investigated and prosecuted. Often, it was due only to the individual initiative of a sympathetic UNHCR staff member, rather than a routine procedure, that cases of sexual and domestic violence were effectively dealt with. In most cases, battered refugee women who lodged complaints of domestic violence with UNHCR were offered only counseling services with an emphasis on reconciling the abused women with their batterers, ignoring the victims' need for safety and justice.[188]

Our research and visits to the Tanzanian camps in May and June 1998 indicated that UNHCR's efforts fell short of what was needed to provide meaningful protection to refugee women in those camps. In addition to the insidious problem of discriminatory attitudes, some of the key problems that Human Rights Watch identified at that time included an insufficient number of protection officers assigned to the Tanzanian camps; lack of clear directions on how to respond to victims of sexual and domestic violence; and too few programs to train UNHCR and its implementing partners' staff, police, prosecutors, magistrates, and other Tanzanian authorities working with refugees on ways to treat victims of sexual and domestic violence.

Some of these problems had been acknowledged by UNHCR and were being addressed during 1998. UNHCR Tanzania subsequently began to tackle other problems as well. In March 1998 UNHCR hired a consultant for five months to assess and work on the issue of sexual violence in the camps in Kasulu, Kibondo, and Ngara regions—the same areas that Human Rights Watch investigated. This consultant issued a report on sexual violence in the camps in these three regions and made efforts to initiate and implement community education projects for refugees in all the camps. UNHCR also held a workshop on sexual violence in Kasulu district

---

[186] Human Rights Watch interview, UNHCR field office head, Kasulu, Tanzania, May 27, 1998.

[187] Human Rights Watch interview, UNHCR protection officer, Kigoma, Tanzania, May 25, 1998.

[188] Human Rights Watch interview, UNHCR field officer, Kibondo, Tanzania, June 3, 1998.

in July 1998. At this workshop, UNHCR staff invited a member of the Tanzania Women Lawyers' Association (TAWLA) to facilitate a workshop to explain Tanzanian laws on rape and physical assault to the participants.[189] In July 1998, a UNHCR junior protection officer was posted to the Kibondo camps, where UNHCR had previously had no protection officer, to carry out protection duties for over 100,000 refugees in those camps. In the first half of 1999, UNHCR deployed a protection officer to the Kasulu camps, bringing the number of protection officers in UNHCR's field offices in Tanzania to four. These four protection officers are responsible for all protection duties in the Kasulu, Ngara, and Kibondo camps: nine refugee camps, with over 500,000 refugees.[190] This is still a daunting task for the protection officers, but it is a marked improvement over what it had been two years earlier.

In February 1999, Human Rights Watch had meetings with a range of officials at UNHCR's headquarters in Geneva. These included staff of the International Protection, Great Lakes Operations, Inspection and Evaluation, Technical and Operational Support, and Programme and Technical Support divisions. The aim was to discuss UNHCR's response to sexual and domestic violence in the Tanzanian refugee camps and how this should be improved. Human Rights Watch argued for better implementation of UNHCR's policy guidelines and programs for refugee women in the camps, including the development of effective programs to combat domestic violence. The director of UNHCR's Great Lakes Operations acknowledged the serious problem posed by domestic and sexual violence in refugee camps and said that UNHCR was planning to strengthen its efforts to prevent such violence through special programs in five sub-Saharan Africa countries: Kenya, Tanzania, Guinea, Liberia, and Sierra Leone.

Developments in 1999

In March 1999, UNHCR launched the Ted Turner Project, which aims to strengthen UNHCR's programs in Kenya, Tanzania, Guinea, Liberia, and Sierra Leone, to prevent sexual and gender-based violence in the camps. In Tanzania, this project—officially known as the Sexual and Gender-Based Violence (SGBV) project, is now at the implementation phase. In each camp, UNHCR protection officers and

---

[189] Human Rights Watch telephone interview, member of Tanzania Women Lawyers Association (TAWLA), Dar-es-Salaam, Tanzania, January 4, 1999.

[190] UNHCR protection officers do not directly carry out protection duties in Lugufu camp. The Lugufu camps in the Kigoma district, housing Congolese refugees, are mainly serviced by Médecins Sans Frontières (Doctors Without Borders), an international humanitarian organization.

community services officers, UNHCR implementing partners, and local NGO staff are creating and coordinating programs to address violence against women in the camps.

- In the Kasulu camps (Mtabila 1 and 2, Muyovosi, and Nyarugusu), the SGBV program is coordinated by the UNHCR protection officer and a protection assistant, the community services officer, the SGBV field assistant,[191] an SGBV lawyer,[192] and staff of UNHCR's implementing partners and local NGOs: Christian Outreach, Africare, and the Diocese of Western Tanganyika.
- In the Kibondo camps (Mtendeli, Kanembwa, Nduta, and Mkugwa) the SGBV program is coordinated by the UNHCR protection officer and a protection assistant, the SGBV coordinator,[193] an SGBV lawyer, and staff of UNHCR's implementing partners and local NGOs: IRC, Dutch Relief Agency, and UMATI.
- In the Ngara camps (Lukole A and B), the SGBV program is coordinated by the UNHCR protection officer and two protection assistants, a community services officer and a community services assistant, and staff of UNHCR's implementing partner, Norwegian People's Aid (NPA).

The SGBV coordinator, lawyers, and field assistant are all new positions funded by the Ted Turner grant. They were recruited by UNHCR on one-year contracts,

---

[191] The SGBV field assistant for the Kasulu camps is a Tanzanian national with a social work background. Her responsibilities include coordinating all community services programs on gender-based violence run by UNHCR and community services implementing partners and local NGOs in the Kasulu camps. The SGBV field assistant works under the supervision of the protection officer.

[192] UNHCR has recruited two Tanzanian lawyers titled SGBV lawyers, based at UNHCR's Kasulu and Kibondo field offices, respectively. The SGBV lawyers are responsible for assisting women victims of rape and other gender-based violence who are willing to pursue their cases in court with legal assistance as well as following up-cases of sexual and gender-based violence reported to the police and court to ensure that cases are properly investigated and prosecuted. The SGBV lawyers work under the supervision of the protection officers.

[193] The SGBV field assistant for the Kibondo camps is a Tanzanian national whose background is in community health and nursing. Her responsibilities include coordinating all community services programs on gender-based violence run by UNHCR and UNHCR community services implementing partners and local NGOs in the Kibondo camps. The SGBV field assistant works under the supervision of the protection officer.

commencing September 1999.[194] The SGBV field assistants and community services officers' responsibilities include following up individual cases of violence against women that require community-based assistance, monitoring and supervising community services programs, and designing a work plan for UNHCR and its implementing partners to ensure coordination, cooperation, and non-duplication of activities.[195] The SGBV lawyers' responsibilities include compiling statistics on all SGBV cases against refugee women in the district and primary courts; following-up and monitoring progress on these cases with the police and courts; intervening with the authorities in individual cases; if appropriate, ensuring that cases are properly investigated and prosecuted; and conducting legal awareness and training workshops for magistrates, prosecutors, UNHCR staff, implementing partners, and refugee leaders and women.[196] UNHCR had no plans, however, at the time of the Human Rights Watch visit, to recruit a lawyer to carry out similar duties in the Ngara camps.[197] The UNHCR protection officers are responsible for overseeing the SGBV program and supervising new staff to ensure that programs are being implemented according to UNHCR's guidelines on protection of refugee women.[198]

In all camps in the Kasulu, Kibondo, and Ngara districts, the SGBV program staff conduct education and awareness sessions on gender-based violence for various components of the refugee community, including refugee men, women, and youth; religious groups; and teachers. The new funding has enabled more community services agencies to participate in the SGBV programs in all camps. Before the launching of the project in 1999, the bulk of the SGBV program activities were carried out in the Kibondo camps by IRC through awareness sessions on sexual and other gender-based violence for refugees and other agency staff. IRC opened drop-in centers in Kanembwa, Mtendeli, Nduta, and Mkugwa camps, each staffed

---

[194] Human Rights Watch interviews, SGBV field assistant, Kasulu, Tanzania, October 29, 1999; SGBV lawyer, Kibondo, Tanzania, November 7, 1999; and SGBV coordinator, Kibondo, Tanzania, November 9, 1999.

[195] Human Rights Watch interviews, UNHCR community services officer, Kasulu, Tanzania, November 2, 1999; SGBV field assistant, Kibondo, Tanzania, November 9, 1999; and UNHCR community services officer, Ngara, Tanzania, November 12, 1999.

[196] Human Rights Watch interview, SGBV lawyer, Kibondo, Tanzania, November 7, 1999.

[197] Human Rights Watch interview, UNHCR protection officer, Ngara, Tanzania, November 11, 1999.

[198] Human Rights Watch interviews, UNHCR protection officer, Kasulu, Tanzania, October 31, 1999; UNHCR associate protection officer, Kibondo, Tanzania, November 9, 1999; and UNHCR protection officer, Ngara, Tanzania, November 9, 1999.

by one national community services officer, a refugee supervisor, and refugee social workers and counselors. The drop-in centers are designed to provide women victims of sexual and gender-based violence with a "safe space" to report their cases and obtain assistance. The staff working at the drop-in centers receive refugees who come to report cases, record cases, and make referrals to UNHCR, the MHA, and other community services and health agencies where victims may request material or health assistance.[199] When refugee victims of sexual and other gender-based violence wish to pursue their cases in court, the IRC staff refer them to UNHCR protection officers.[200]

With funding from the Ted Turner Project, UNHCR's implementing partner, UMATI, took over from IRC the programs on sexual and other gender-based violence in the Kanembwa and Mkugwa camps.[201] In Mtendeli camp, the Dutch Relief Agency and IRC share the running of community services programs, with the aim of increasing their capacity to respond to these problems in the refugee camps.[202] IRC is now solely coordinating the SGBV program in only one camp: Nduta.[203] UNHCR implementing partners and local NGOs in Kasulu (Africare, Christian Outreach, and the Diocese of Western Tanzania) have begun to provide services to refugees in the Kasulu camps that are similar to the services provided at IRC's drop-in centers in the Kibondo camps.[204] As of November 1999, UNHCR and community services implementing partners in Kasulu expected to expand existing community services buildings to include permanent drop-in centers fashioned after the IRC drop-in centers in the Kibondo camps.[205]

---

[199] Human Rights Watch interview, IRC community services officers, Kibondo, Tanzania, November 5, 1999.

[200] Human Rights Watch interview, IRC community services officers, Kibondo, Tanzania, November 5, 1999.

[201] Human Rights Watch interview, UMATI community services officer, Kibondo, Tanzania, November 9, 1999.

[202] Human Rights Watch interview, Dutch Relief Agency community services officers, Kibondo, Tanzania, November 6, 1999.

[203] Human Rights Watch interview, IRC community services officers, Kibondo, Tanzania, November 6, 1999.

[204] Human Rights Watch interviews, Christian Outreach community services coordinator, Kasulu, Tanzania, October 27, 1999; Africare community services officers, Kasulu, Tanzania, October 28, 1999; and UNHCR community services officer, Kasulu, Tanzania, November 2, 1999.

[205] Ibid.

In the Ngara camps (Lukole A and B), UNHCR community services officers and UNHCR's implementing partner, Norwegian People's Aid, have established women's centers that provide services similar to IRC's drop in centers in Kibondo. UNHCR community services and Norwegian People's Aid have organized refugee committees to form crisis intervention teams, which include refugee men and women, to attend to victims who come to report cases at the women's centers in the Ngara camps. UNHCR and Norwegian People's Aid also coordinate programs to raise community awareness on sexual violence and to mainstream women's participation in leadership and education. These education and awareness programs focus on all women in Lukole A and B camps, especially those in positions of leadership, such as women representatives and counselors. UNHCR has placed a female teacher in each of the eleven primary schools in Ngara camps to focus on creating awareness of sexual violence and other problems affecting refugee girls in the schools. Additionally, community services officers and four trained refugee women in the Ngara camps provide post-trauma counseling to victims of sexual attacks.[206]

Overall, UNHCR's sexual and other gender-based violence programs in Tanzania have laid a solid foundation for achieving security for refugee women in those camps. With time, consistent monitoring, and the adoption of new strategies to strengthen these programs, women refugees in the Tanzanian camps will have much needed protection against gender-based violence in the camps.

The Refugee-Run Community Justice System

UNHCR's policy on the protection of refugee women encourages UNHCR staff to improve the standards of internal dispute resolution mechanisms within refugee camps in order to ensure that protection problems affecting women refugees are covered and that women have equal access to the remedies provided by these structures. Section 51 of the *Guidelines on Refugee Women*, reads, "UNHCR staff should review legal codes and processes adopted in the camps to make sure that protection needs of women refugees are covered and that women have equal access to the remedies provided in these courts. Encourage adoption of rules governing these situations, encourage the participation of refugee women in these procedures, and provide training to those administering them."[207] These refugee-run structures are not state-sanctioned courts of law, but rather operate as a community justice

---

[206] Human Rights Watch interviews, Norwegian People's Aid community services officers, Ngara, Tanzania, November 11, 1999 and UNHCR community services officer, Ngara, Tanzania, November 12, 1999.

[207] Section 51, *Guidelines on Refugee Women*, p. 35.

system run by refugees to resolve disputes among themselves. In the Tanzanian camps, a refugee-run informal justice system based on Burundian custom co-exists with the Tanzanian criminal justice system. However, the lack of enforcement powers leaves the refugee-run system in no position to deliver justice to victims. Moreover, without monitoring or guidance and training on how to deal with cases, particularly cases of domestic and sexual violence, the refugee-run system tends not to meet the needs of women victims of violence in the camps.

The Burundian traditional system of justice utilizes customary practices for handling disputes, and it has been transplanted to the refugee setting. It consists mainly of elder male refugees, who mediate and reconcile people who are having problems—ranging from disputes between husbands and wives to disagreements between neighbors, and parents and children. To be recognized as a *mushingatahe* (member of the abashingatahe) under Burundian custom, an individual needs to be a person of integrity and to earn the respect and confidence of the community.

The abashingatahe form a traditional council, which regularly presides over offenses such as theft, domestic violence, and other assault cases and functions largely as a reconciliatory body.[208] The sanctions the abashingatahe may impose are therefore minor, even for serious offenses like domestic violence.[209] A refugee mushingatahe in Kanembwa camp told Human Rights Watch that, according to Burundian custom, the abashingatahe are not supposed to impose monetary fines as punishment for any case, but in the refugee setting that has been changed. In cases of domestic violence, a husband who beats his wife is required by the council to "apologize" formally to his wife by buying her a piece of cloth. However, in the Tanzanian refugee camps, we found that the abashingatahe often imposed small fines of around one thousand Tanzanian shillings (approximately U.S.$2.00) on alleged perpetrators of domestic violence, who then received no further sanction.[210] Many refugees fail to pay even this fine, thus suffering no consequences for their crime as the traditional councils have no power to enforce their rulings.

Some refugees expressed the view that the traditional councils offered a chance of securing some form of redress, compared to the inadequate Tanzanian criminal justice system. Moreover, the role of the abashingatahe is more acceptable to some refugee women who wish to pursue a reconciliatory approach rather than have their

[208] Human Rights Watch interview, Nicodeme L., mushingatahe, Kanembwa camp, Tanzania, June 3, 1998.

[209] Human Rights Watch interview, Paul Z., mushingatahe, Kanembwa camp, June 3, 1998.

[210] Human Rights Watch interview, IRC Gender-Based Sexual Violence Project coordinator, Kibondo, Tanzania, June 1, 1998.

husbands prosecuted in court.   However, some domestic violence victims complained to Human Rights Watch that the abashingatahe did nothing to punish their batterers and that their batterers never complied with the judgements given by the abashingatahe.[211] Jeanne Y., whose domestic violence case is cited above, was beaten several times by her husband for failing to give birth to more children. She reported the case, and the abashingatahe warned her husband not to beat her again. Yet Jeanne Y.'s husband ignored the warning and continued to beat her.[212]

Much of the refugees' frustration stems from the abashingatahe's lack of enforcement powers and the low priority they attach to protecting women victims of domestic violence, which is invariably treated as a "lesser crime."

The lack of satisfactory redress through either the Tanzanian legal system or the refugee-run justice system underscores the urgent need for UNHCR to strengthen preventive measures and to improve recourse to justice when domestic violence occurs. Greater effort should be made to guide and monitor the abashingatahe when they deal with domestic disputes; to ensure that all cases of violence are referred for criminal investigation; to train abashingatahe on women's rights; to establish safe places for victims of domestic violence in the camps; and to make the Tanzanian criminal justice system more accessible to women refugees who wish to pursue cases of domestic violence against them through the courts.

---

[211] Human Rights Watch interview, Rosalie P., Mtendeli camp, Tanzania, June 3, 1998. This case is described fully under the "Domestic Violence" section.

[212] Human Rights Watch interview, Jeanne Y., Mtendeli camp, Tanzania, June 3, 1998.

IX. CONCLUSION

Women's vulnerability to human rights abuses in Tanzania's refugee camps is compounded by the lack of adequate assistance to those camps. In refugee situations like those in Africa, where international focus on and assistance to refugees is particularly limited, the resource scarcity impacts most severely on vulnerable women and children. These groups face the greatest challenge to securing both the basic necessities for life and the rights and freedoms which they should enjoy even as refugees. As the evidence from Tanzania shows, the failure to provide necessary assistance to refugees in Africa and to ensure that such aid is available to women opens the way to serious, ongoing human rights violations. It is vitally important, therefore, that UNHCR has now initiated programs to address sexual and domestic violence in the Tanzanian refugee camps. These initiatives are evidence that, with staff training and resources, much can be done to afford necessary protection to refugee women. While UNHCR's current programs to protect women refugees from violence in the Tanzanian camps are in their initial stages and will take some time to affect the lives of refugee women, they are steps in the right direction and, if ultimately successful, could and should be adapted and replicated in UNHCR programs elsewhere.

UNHCR's *Guidelines on Refugee Women* clearly observe that women's protection needs must be addressed from the very earliest stages of an emergency, stating, "Decisions made early in a refugee emergency regarding such fundamental issues as camp lay-out and food distribution mechanisms can have long-term ramifications for the protection of refugee women."[213] Similarly, the *Sexual Violence Guidelines* underscore the importance of taking appropriate preventive measures in the early stages of a refugee crisis, noting that "mistakes in the early phases of the creation of a camp are extremely difficult to correct satisfactorily later."[214]

There are several important lessons that can be drawn from the Tanzania case. First, UNHCR needs to ensure an institutionalized response to address the protection needs of refugee women from the onset of any emergency, rather than waiting until a problem has been identified to respond. Second, UNHCR guidelines on the protection of refugee women and the prevention of sexual violence must be speedily and consistently implemented in all refugee situations, and UNHCR staff need to be fully apprized of and trained on their content. Third, UNHCR must address the

---

[213] UNHCR, *Guidelines on Refugee Women*, p. 15.

[214] UNHCR, *Sexual Violence Guidelines*, p. 12.

protection gap for victims of domestic violence and urgently introduce policy guidelines for its staff on how to prevent and respond to the problem of domestic violence. Fourth, from the onset of any refugee emergency, UNHCR must work closely with the host government wherever possible, to ensure that cases of sexual and domestic violence against refugee women are properly investigated and prosecuted, under the host government's laws. Finally, the Tanzanian case illustrates that with institutional commitment and adequate support, many of the protection needs of refugee women can be effectively addressed by UNHCR.

SEXUAL VIOLENCE AGAINST REFUGEES
GUIDELINES ON PREVENTION AND RESPONSE
Geneva 1995

FOREWORD

Sexual violence against refugees is a global problem. It constitutes a violation of basic human rights, instilling fear in the lives of victims already profoundly affected by their displacement. Refugees from Bosnia and Herzegovina, Rwanda, Somalia and Vietnam have brought with them harrowing stories of abuse and suffering.

How can the international community prevent sexual violence? How should we respond if a woman becomes pregnant as a result of being raped? What should we do if a child has been sexually attacked? There are no simple answers to these questions.

An understanding of the ways in which sexual violence affects victims will assist those working with them to help alleviate their suffering. The UNHCR Guidelines on Preventing and Responding to Sexual Violence Against Refugees provide a primer on when and how sexual violence can occur in the refugee context and the physical, psychological and social effects it can have on those exposed.

These Guidelines highlight the fact that many, and perhaps most, incidents of sexual violence remain unreported for reasons including shame, social stigma and fear of reprisal or the case going to trial.

The Guidelines address ways to combat the occurrence of sexual violence and how to respond when incidents occur. They emphasize the need for education, training and information campaigns. The Guidelines underline the need for refugees, and in particular refugee women, to receive legal awareness training, leadership and skills training, and education.

I recommend the use of these UNHCR Guidelines on Preventing and Responding to Sexual Violence Against Refugees to field workers and others who come into contact with refugees. I hope they will serve as a useful guide and lead to a greater understanding of this widespread and very sensitive issue.

Radhika Coomaraswamy
Special Rapporteur on violence against women
Commission on Human Rights
Colombo, 8 March 1995

PREFACE

Sexual violence against refugees is widespread. Women and young girls and, less frequently, men and boys are vulnerable to attack, both during their flight and while in exile. They are vulnerable from many quarters and in every case, the physical and psychological trauma that results can only add to the pain of displacement and the bitterness of exile.

UNHCR, which has been mandated to protect and assist refugees worldwide, is acutely aware of the dimensions of the problem. The following guidelines for preventing and responding to sexual violence against refugees are intended to promote more effective ways for all concerned parties to act and react. The intention is to provide UNHCR, non-governmental organizations and other field workers with basic practical advice in areas of medical treatment, psychological support, and legal intervention.

I wish to thank all those who shared valuable comments during the production of these Guidelines. I hope they will make an important contribution to strengthening the efforts of UNHCR, our implementing partners, and host governments to prevent sexual violence and provide more sympathetic and effective responses to this global outrage.

Sadako Ogata
United Nations High Commissioner for Refugees
Geneva, 8 March 1995

INTRODUCTION

Background

Refugee workers assisting victims of sexual violence have long needed guidelines. Initially, guidelines were drawn up for use in asylum camps in South-East Asia. Subsequent events in the former Yugoslavia, Kenya and Rwanda have renewed attention to this need. The Guidelines begin by defining sexual violence, where it may occur, its causes and effects, and outlining reasons why many incidents remain unreported.

The second chapter suggests a range of preventive measures that can and should be taken involving the refugees themselves, as well as those responsible for their care.

The third and fourth chapters deal respectively with practical measures to be taken in response to incidents of sexual violence, and with the legal aspects. The final chapter offers guidance on media interest, female genital mutilation and staff trauma.

A checklist of the practical measures suggested is included in Annex 1. A Sexual Violence Needs Assessment and Programme Framework tool is provided in Annex 5.

The Guidelines are intended to assist all staff, particularly in the field, who are concerned with providing protection and assistance to refugees. Addressing protection is the responsibility of all UNHCR staff members. While some staff have professional skills which make them particularly qualified to deal with protection matters, the extent of the problem requires all staff to understand, and to master basic skills in addressing it. UNHCR hopes that the Guidelines will be useful not only to our own staff, but also to the staff of other United Nations bodies, intergovernmental and non-governmental organizations and national governmental agencies working with refugees. These Guidelines have been drafted for use in a broad range of cultural and political contexts.

Aim

The Guidelines provide basic advice on appropriate action, particularly preventive, and are also intended to encourage active reflection and discussion between colleagues. They seek to promote attitudinal changes in relation to sexual violence where these are an obstacle, to improve or initiate services that address psychosocial as well as health needs, and, overall, to create an awareness and sensitivity to the special needs and concerns of refugees who have been subjected to sexual violence. While they indicate the type of referral or action required, they are not a do-it-yourself handbook f for areas in which specialized care is needed.

Terminology
Focus on females
The pronouns in these Guidelines in relation to victims of sexual violence are phrased in the feminine voice and the pronouns in , relation to perpetrators of sexual violence are phrased in the masculine voice. This is in recognition of the fact that the majority of reported cases of sexual violence among refugees involve female victims and male perpetrators. Since women and girls appear to be the ones most often subjected to sexual violence, these Guidelines focus on sexual violence against female refugees. Very little is known about the true incidence of sexual violence against male refugees other than in the context of detention and torture.

"Refugees" and "refugee camps"
For the sake of convenience, "refugees" refers also to asylum seekers, returnees and to internally displaced persons ("IDPs") protected or assisted by UNHCR.

Similarly, "refugee camps" refers also to reception centres or places of detention for asylum-seekers, or centres for IDPs.

The Guidelines apply with the necessary changes being made to asylum-seekers, returnees and IDPs.

The term "victim"
Although the term "victim" is used in these Guidelines, the stigmatization and perceived powerlessness associated with being a "victim" should be avoided by all concerned parties. While victims require compassion and sensitivity, their strength and resilience should also be recognized and borne in mind.

Applicability
Certain guidance will not apply or may be difficult to implement due to the limited capacity and resources available. Nonetheless, use of these Guidelines to the greatest extent possible is encouraged.

Each refugee situation is different and the manner and extent to which these Guidelines apply may differ depending on:
- the cultural context
- whether camp or urban
- the caseload
- available resources
- the legal system.

CHAPTER 1: SEXUAL VIOLENCE IN THE CONTEXT OF REFUGEES

1.1 Definition and Nature of Sexual Violence

Sexual violence is a gross violation of fundamental human rights and, when committed in the context of armed conflict, a grave breach of humanitarian law.

> *Not[es] with grave concern the widespread*
> *occurrence of sexual violence in violation of*
> *the fundamental right to personal security as*
> *recognized in international human rights and*
> *humanitarian law, which inflicts serious harm*
> *and injury to the victims, their families and*
> *communities, and which has been a cause of*
> *coerced displacement including refugee*
> *movements in some areas of the world,...*

Executive Committee Conclusion No. 73 (XLIV) (1993), Preamble
Refugee Protection and Sexual Violence

There are various forms of sexual violence, rape being the one most commonly referred to. The legal definition of rape varies from country to country. In many societies it is defined as sexual intercourse with another person without their consent. Rape is committed when the victim's resistance is overcome by force or fear or under other coercive conditions. In certain countries "statutory rape" exists as an offense. This is sexual intercourse with someone under a specified age, which is deemed to be unlawful. The victim is presumed by law to be unable to give consent by reason of his or her tender age.

However, many forms of sexual violence do not fall under the strict definition of rape, such as insertion of objects into genital openings, oral and anal coitus, attempted rape and the infliction of other sexually abusive acts. Sexual violence can also involve the use or threat of force in order to have sexual acts performed by third persons.

The term "sexual violence" is used in these Guidelines to cover all forms of sexual threat, assault, interference and exploitation, including "statutory rape" and molestation without physical harm or penetration.

Perpetrators of sexual violence are often motivated by a desire for power and domination. Given these motivating forces, rape is common in situations of armed conflict and internal strife. An act of forced sexual behaviour can be life-threatening. Like other forms of torture, it is often meant to hurt, control and humiliate, violating a person's innermost physical and mental integrity.

Perpetrators of sexual violence can include family members, for example where a parent is sexually abusing a child. Domestic violence often escalates in refugee situations due to the enormous pressures of refugee life, for example, having to live in closed camps.

1.2 Persons Most Vulnerable to Sexual Violence

Experience shows that unaccompanied women and lone female heads of household are at the greatest risk of being subjected to sexual violence. Children are particularly vulnerable to sexual abuse given their high level of trust. Unaccompanied children and children in foster families also are especially at risk. Furthermore, refugees of all ages and both genders face a significantly increased risk of sexual violence when in detention or detention-like situations. Refugee workers should be aware that the very old, the infirm, and the physically and mentally disabled may also be vulnerable to attack.

Refugees most at risk of being subjected to sexual violence:
- unaccompanied women
- lone female heads of household
- unaccompanied children
- children in foster care arrangements
- those in detention or detention-like situations.

1.3 Situations Where Sexual Violence May Occur

> *Not[es] also distressing reports that refugees and asylum-seekers, including children, in many instances have been subjected to rape or other forms of sexual violence during their flight or following their arrival in countries where they sought asylum, including sexual extortion in connection with the granting of basic necessities, personal documentation or refugee status,...*

Executive Committee Conclusion No. 73 (XLIV) (1993), Preamble
Refugee Protection and Sexual Violence

The following are some situations in which sexual violence against refugees has been known to occur:

a) Prior to flight

Men, women and children may be targeted for abuse by the police, the military or other officials in the country of origin. Individuals may be detained, which heightens the risk of sexual violence and torture. Sexual violence may also occur at the hands of irregular forces in situations of internal conflict. Sexual violence may even occur with the complicity of male leaders, in the form of bartering women or girls for arms and ammunition or other benefits.

b) During flight

Refugees may be sexually attacked by pirates, bandits, members of the security forces, smugglers or other refugees. Border guards may detain and abuse women and girls, sometimes for extended periods; pirates may capture women as they travel by boat and extort sex in exchange fol their safety and onward passage. Smugglers may assist female refugees across the border in exchange for sex and/or money and valuables.

c) In the country of asylum

The country of asylum does not necessarily provide sanctuary from sexual violence. Whether refugees live in camps or in urban situations, they may be subjected to sexual attacks by persons in authority or otherwise in a position to take advantage of their particularly vulnerable situation. In a variety of asylum situations, officials who determine the refugee status of the applicant may extort sex in exchange for a positive determination. Refugee women and girls may be approached for sexual favours in exchange for assistance, such as during food distribution. Unaccompanied children, in particular girls, placed in foster care may suffer sexual abuse by the foster family members.

Refugees may be sexually attacked by members of the local population, by officials, including those responsible for their protection such as border guards, police or military personnel, by international refugee workers, or by fellow refugees. Forms of domestic violence often escalate in direct proportion to the pressures of refugee life.

Sexual attacks may occur while women go about daily chores, particularly if these involve visiting isolated areas. Attacks can take place at night in the homes of victims and in front of family members or an individual may be abducted and sexually violated away from her home. Armed assailants may attack in groups, converging on a camp. In extreme situations, some refugees, who initially fled their country of origin due to internal conflict, have been known to return home in order to seek relief from the general insecurity existing in the country of asylum.

In addition, coercive prostitution, or the exploitation of the prostitution of women and girls by camp officials in collaboration with local prostitution rings may also occur.

d) During repatriation operations

Where large population movements may separate women and girls from their usual support systems, crowding and other changes may make normal control and protection measures difficult to implement. The same dangers found during flight and exile may be faced once again on the return journey or upon return in the country of origin.

e) During reintegration phases

Returned refugees may be targeted by the Government, military or others in retribution for having fled. Women in particular may be susceptible to sexual extortion in exchange for material assistance or for identification cards or other forms of documentation required by government officials.

1.4 Under-Reporting of Sexual Violence

The true scale of sexual violence against refugees is unknown because numerous incidents are never reported.

There is a risk that refugee workers and officials will deny the existence of sexual violence because incidents are not reported. It is essential to be aware that the problem may exist, and to adapt reporting and interviewing techniques to encourage people to report incidents. (More guidance on this is given below). Reporting and follow-up must be done in a highly sensitive and confidential manner, in order not to cause further suffering or further danger to lives.

Reasons for under-reporting may include the following:

Negative consequences of reporting
- In most cultures and communities, sexual attacks are perceived as shameful. and the victims are stigmatized. In some societies, the chastity and virginity of women reflect on the honour of the family.
- The experience of sexual violence in such a cultural context is therefore not only devastating physically, emotionally, intellectually, and

psychologically, but may lead to the woman û and her family û being ostracized by the community. She may be unable to marry or to stay married. In certain societies, a woman who has been raped may be perceived as the culprit, and consequently may be liable to punishment.

Where the negative consequences of reporting sexual violence can include ostracism the disintegration of a family, detention and trial, stigmatization, or further attacks by the perpetrators, there is a strong likelihood of under-reporting of sexual violence.

Male victims' reluctance to report

- When men or boys are victims of sexual violence, some of these problems can be compounded. While at least some legal and social networks, however rudimentary, often exist for women and girls who have been sexually attacked, there is rarely anything comparable for male victims.
- Men may experience profound humiliation, taking the assault as a slur on their virility or manhood.
- In many societies men are discouraged from talking about their emotions and may find it very difficult to acknowledge and describe what has happened to them.

For these reasons, it is suspected that the reported cases of sexual violence against males are a fraction of the true number of cases.

Personal discomfort of refugee workers or officials

- Refugee workers, community leaders or officials may avoid confronting, remedying and preventing acts of sexual violence because of their personal discomfort with the subject. They may also fear that raising the issue with the Government could damage relations or their own image.   While it is hoped that these Guidelines and/or receiving training may help dispel the personal discomfort of refugee workers, sexual violence is an intrinsically disturbing subject which often provokes strong emotional responses. It is essential to overcome the resistance, whether of ourselves or our counterparts, to discuss the problem frankly and openly.

Dismissal by refugee workers or officials as a private matter

- The discomfort which refugee workers or officials may feel about sexual violence can be aggravated by a tendency to dismiss it as a purely private matter, or as an inevitable by-product of the situation. This shows a lack of awareness. It is important to understand that sexual violence is a serious violation of an individual'spersonal security and integrity. It is UNHCR's responsibility to ensure protection and assistance.

Additional reasons for non-reporting
- Reluctance of the authorities in many countries to identify and prosecute the assailants.
- Inability of the refugee to speak the local language, or to report to officers of the same gender.
- Fear of reprisals in circumstances when the violence was perpetrated by someone in authority, such as a camp guard; anonymity in refugee situations may, to some, offer greater protection.

1.5 Effects of Sexual Violence

Sexual violence can have serious physical, social, intellectual and psychological consequences. Professional medical, legal and psychosocial care is required. Reactions are likely to vary considerably depending on the victim's age, gender, personality, prior sexual experience, cultural background, and the availability of a support network.

Physical consequences
- The physical consequences of sexual violence may include HIV infection, sexually transmitted diseases, mutilated genitalia, pregnancy, miscarriage of an existing foetus, abortion, menstrual disorder, severe abdominal pain and self-mutilation as a result of psychological trauma.
- Where women and girls have undergone extreme forms of female genital mutilation, they may suffer extensive injuries if their genitalia are reopened by a sharp instrument or by the force of penetration itself.

Psychological consequences
- Even if physical injury is minimal, all victims experience psychological trauma. They may feel paralyzed by terror, experience physical and emotional pain, intense self-disgust, powerlessness, worthlessness, apathy, denial and an inability to function in their daily lives. In the worst cases they may experience deep depression leading to chronic mental disorders, suicide, illegal termination of pregnancy, endangering their lives, or abandonment of their babies. Cases of infanticide of children born as a result of rape have also been reported.

For further discussion see 3.9 (a) Common Psychological Reactions.

Social consequences
- As noted in 1.4 above, the social consequences of sexual violence can range from rejection by the spouse and immediate family members, to stigmatization or ostracism by the community, further sexual exploitation, and/or severe punishment. They can also include deprivation of education, employment and other types of assistance and protection.

It is therefore extremely important to be aware of signs of sexual violence and to investigate discreetly if there is any suspicion that an individual may have been subjected to it. Such investigation must be done in a sensitive and sympathetic way with complete respect for confidentiality. See 3.3 Identifying Incidents of Sexual Violence.

1.6 Causes of Sexual Violence

Section 1.3 above describes situations in which incidents of sexual violence may occur. From this knowledge it is possible to extrapolate the following causes and/or circumstances which allow sexual attacks to take place.

a) Society (of refugees, and surroundings)
- Sexual violence in the country of origin may have a political motive, for example where mass rape of populations is used to dominate, control and/or uproot, or where sexual torture is used as a method of interrogation. Sometimes sexual violence is used as a weapon of warfare, to humiliate or cause the disintegration of another community, as a part of "ethnic cleansing".
- Attacks by neighbouring groups may occur in areas where refugees are considered materially privileged compared with the local population. Within camps, women who are economically successful have been targeted.
- Attacks by the local population because of the consequences flowing from refugee presence, such as fear of criminal activities, racism, xenophobia and other concerns including degradation of the environment and depletion of natural resources.
- Traditional tensions and feuds between various clans/groups may also give rise to sexual violence.

- The collapse of traditional societal support mechanisms (social sanctions, norms for proper behaviour, etc.) when refugees were forced to flee or to live in camp surroundings. In particular, the communal support systems for the protection of vulnerable individuals may no longer be present, for example, due to the absence of many male members from the community.
- Male attitudes of disrespect towards women may be instrumental in causing incidents of sexual violence. For example, camp guards and male refugees may look upon unaccompanied women and girls in refugee camps as common sexual property. Husbands or other male family members may also abuse a victim of a previous attack because they believe she is no longer "virtuous".
- Psychological strain on refugee men in not being able to assume normal cultural, social and economic roles, may cause aggressive behaviour towards women. Many other aspects of refugee life can aggravate this, including idleness, anger at loss of control and power, uncertainty about the future, and frustration with living conditions.
- Alcohol and drug abuse can result in violent behaviour within families and communities. Such abuse is often linked to boredom. depression and stress.

b) Vulnerability

- Sexual violence during flight or in the country of asylum can occur because of the special vulnerability and powerlessness of refugees, including the need for "safe" passage. This is underlined by the common misconception held by people who come into contact with refugees, such as members of the military and police, that they are not legally protected outside their country of origin.
- Females who are on their own for whatever reason, whether they are single, widowed, abandoned, unaccompanied minors, lone heads of households, or women who have been separated from male family members by the chaos of flight or during voluntary repatriation, are all particularly at risk of sexual violence.
- Where foster care placement of children occurs without proper screening of families or monitoring of the child's welfare, the refugee child may be exposed to sexual abuse.
- Incarceration in closed detention facilities may compound the problems of sexual violence. In a number of countries, all individuals who enter illegally or without authorization are subject to detention regardless of

age, sex, or their status as asylum-seekers. In some cases, asylum applicants are incarcerated with criminals, children with unrelated adults, females with males.

- Refugee women without proper personal documentation are susceptible to sexual exploitation and abuse. In many refugee situations, women are not routinely provided with documents showing that they are legally in the country. The male family member may have been designated as the head of household and given the relevant documents; he may not be present to produce these documents before the authorities as and when required. Similarly, refugee women may not be given individual registration cards or documents with which they collect food rations, shelter material and qualify for other forms of assistance.
- Male responsibility for distribution of goods and necessities may expose women to sexual exploitation. In camps where male authorities or male refugees have this responsibility, women may be coerced into sexual acts. For example sexual favours may be demanded in exchange for food rations.

c) Camp design and location
- The geographical location of a refugee camp may increase the likelihood of sexual violence, if the camp is located in an area which has a serious crime problem for example, or is geographically isolated from the local population.
- The design and social structure in many refugee camps and settlements may contribute to the likelihood of protection problems. Camps are often overcrowded. Unrelated families may need to share communal living and sleeping space. In effect, such refugees are living among strangers. perhaps among persons who could be considered traditional enemies.
- Poor design of services and facilities may also contribute to security problems. Communal latrines and washing facilities may be at some distance from the living quarters, thereby increasing the potential for attacks. Many camps are not lit, or poorly lit, compounding these risks at night. Night patrols exist in some camps, but not in others. The distance refugees must travel to food, water and fuel distribution points or collection areas may also expose them to danger. Also, where refugees are housed in centres and camps, sleeping rooms and washing facilities usually cannot be locked.
- The lack of police protection and general lawlessness in some camps is also a factor. Police may accept bribes in exchange for not investigating

complaints, or for releasing the alleged perpetrators from custody. Police officers, military personnel, camp administrators or other government officers may themselves be involved in acts of abuse or exploitation.

d) UNHCR/Other presence

- The lack of UNHCR or NGO access to, or presence in, camps, particularly at night can be a contributing factor. The absence of an independent presence in camps is thought likely to increase the risks of attacks on personal security, including sexual violence. At the same time, the security situation might not allow for this presence.

1.7 False Claims

One should not overlook the possibility, even though remote, that reports of sexual violence may be fabricated for a variety of reasons, for example, to bring undesirable repercussions to others in the course of domestic or inter-community disputes, for financial gain, or to advance resettlement prospects.

CHAPTER 2: PREVENTIVE MEASURES

Recogniz[es] the need for concrete action to detect, deter and redress instances of sexual violence to effectively protect asylum-seekers and refugees,

Recogniz[es] further that the prevention of sexual violence can contribute to averting coerced displacement including refugee situations and to facilitating solutions,...

Executive Committee Conclusion No. 73 (XLIV) (1993), Preamble
Refugee Protection and Sexual Violence

"Prevention is better than cure"
States have primary responsibility for ensuring the physical protection of refugees within their territory. UNHCR's role in providing international protection most often involves ensuring that Governments take the necessary action to protect the refugees within their territory.

All possible measures must be taken to prevent the occurrence of sexual violence. First, the nature of the risks with which the refugees may be confronted must be assessed (see 1.6 Causes of Sexual Violence above). UNHCR representatives, in collaboration with other relevant UN bodies and agencies, host Governments and NGOs, should make every effort to ensure that the following measures are implemented to prevent sexual violence from occurring.

> *Urges States, relevant United Nations organizations as well as non-governmental organizations, as appropriate, to... integrate considerations specific to the protection of refugee women into assistance activities from their inception, including when planning refugee camps and settlements, in order to be able to deter, detect and redress instances of physical and sexual abuse as well as other protection concerns at the earliest possible moment.*

Executive Committee Conclusion No. 64 (XLI) (1990), paragraph (a) (v)
Refugee Women and International Protection

> *Urges States to take all measures necessary to prevent or remove threats to the personal security of refugees and asylum-seekers in border areas and elsewhere, including by affording UNHCR*

> *and, as appropriate, other organizations approved by the*
> *Governments concerned prompt and unhindered access to them,*
> *by situating refugee camps and settlements in secure locations,*
> *by ensuring the safety of vulnerable groups, by facilitating the*
> *issuance of personal documentation, and by involving the refugee*
> *community, both women and men. in the organization and*
> *administration of their camps and settlements.*

Executive Committee Conclusion No. 72 (XLIV) (1993), paragraph (b)
Personal Security of Refugees

2.1 Preventive Measures involving Refugees and Refugee Workers

Refugee workers can take a number of important practical steps to reduce the risk of sexual violence. However, it is important to note that the most effective measures require the refugee community to play a prominent role, actively participating in promoting self-protection. Close liaison with the local authorities is also of paramount importance.

a) Design and location of refugee camps

Mistakes in the early phases of the creation of a camp are extremely difficult to correct satisfactorily later.

Ensure that the physical design and location of refugee camps enhances, rather than undermines, their physical security. Layout and organization of the camps and facilities are determining factors in the protection of refugees. Every effort should be made to encourage the refugee community to identify and provide the appropriate solutions to such problems.

Special measures which may need to be implemented to reduce exposure to risk:

Geographical location
- Avoid the establishment of camps within close proximity to the border of the country of origin, or in areas that are unsafe, e.g., subject to banditry.

Design and social structure
- Consult with the refugees, and other sources if possible, to understand their preferred physical and social organization, and seek to replicate it in the camp, ensuring in particular that women are involved in this process.

- Conserve the original community, to the extent possible, from the country of origin within the new site.
- Provide for special accommodation (e.g. specially secured housing) for unaccompanied women and girls and lone female heads of household in full consultation with them. For instance, accommodate single women with sufficient security personnel on guard. Remember to ensure adequate security when vulnerable individuals are grouped together, since they could become a target for attack.
- Attempt to ensure that unrelated families do not share communal living and sleeping space.

Services and facilities
- Improve lighting where possible, particularly on the paths used by women at night for access to services and facilities.
- Ensure, where practical, that women and girls are able to lock their sleeping and washing facilities.
- Ensure that basic services and facilities at camps are located in such a manner that refugee women do not become exposed to attack. For instance, build latrines at a distance from huts which enables women to use them safely at night.

b) Security patrols
- Encourage patrols of security personnel by foot and vehicle during the day and/or at night, as appropriate.
- Form refugee security patrols or small vigilance groups, preferably by trusted members of the refugee community, to guard at night, with the protection of refugee women as a first priority. In some camps, refugees have done so by shouting and banging cooking pots and pans to draw attention to and scare away attackers.

c) Provision of protective materials
- Where appropriate, provide communities with materials which can assist them in protecting themselves, such as fencing or barbed wire. The experience in some remote refugee camps showed that night bandit attacks reduced dramatically when sections of the camps were fenced off, using thorn bushes.

d) Promote alternatives to closed camps

- Identify and promote alternatives to camps where possible, particularly alternatives to closed camps and detention centres. Prolonged stay in camps can lead to a breakdown in law and order.

e) Where incarceration occurs

Note[s] with deep concern that large numbers of refugees and asylum-seekers in different areas of the world are currently the subject of detention or similar restrictive measures by reason of their illegal entry or presence in search of asylum, pending resolution of their situation,

Express[es] the opinion that in view of the hardship which it involves, detention should normally be avoided,

Executive Committee Conclusion No. 44 (XXXVII) (1986), paragraphs (a) and (b) Detention of Refugees and Asylum-Seekers

- UNHCR should always seek to ensure that asylum-seekers are not detained. Where individual asylum-seekers are, nonetheless, detained upon entry, insist that they are not incarcerated with criminals and that women are not with males, unless they are together with male family members.
- It is UNHCR's policy that refugee children should not be detained. Due to the harmful effects detention may have, it must be "used only as a measure of last resort and for the shortest appropriate period of time". (Convention on the Rights of the Child, article 37(b)).

f) Camp meetings and plan of action

- Bearing in mind cultural sensitivities, hold camp meetings between UNHCR, NGOs, police, military and other relevant government officers to discuss the problem of sexual violence. Such discussions could form part of the regular interagency meetings or be addressed in security meetings where such meetings take place. In particular, possible causes should be analyzed and a strategy to address and prevent incidents formulated. An inter-agency plan of action could be developed for implementation of these Guidelines and to clarify roles and activities in addressing this issue.
- Ensure that refugees and particularly representatives from refugee women's groups participate in discussions on this issue and have the opportunity to speak about any special needs they may have. When necessary, for example where women feel inhibited or uneasy discussing matters in the presence of male refugees, separate meetings should be held

for women and for men. Make use of such fora to explain UNHCR's protection role, in particular regarding prevention of sexual violence.

g) Involvement of female refugees

- In many camps, the leadership structure is dominated by male refugees. It is important that the involvement of more female leaders be encouraged and the role and responsibilities of women be broadened and strengthened. The establishment of refugee women's committees and groups is important to represent the interests of women in the camp, and UNHCR should play an active role in promoting this.

h) Specific focus on vulnerable individuals

- Identify individuals or groups who may be particularly vulnerable to violence, e.g., lone female heads of household with disabled family members, or women who are economically successful, and develop appropriate strategies to address their particular protection and assistance problems.

i) Preempt any retaliation

- Experience has shown that retaliatory violence can erupt following an incident in which refugees, the local community, outside attackers or security personnel have been killed or injured. Where retaliation can be anticipated, increased security measures should be adopted. This may include warning refugees to take extra precautions (such as to remain indoors), requesting the deployment of additional security forces and/or securing greater UNHCR presence in the field.

j) UNHCR access to detainees

- UNHCR must have direct and unhindered access to detainees to monitor their safety and conditions. Access to police holding cells or prisons may be important to prevent sexual violence from occurring in detention. Where refugees have been placed in police custody on suspicion of or having been charged with committing a crime, it may be necessary to visit the refugees to ensure their well being and humane treatment. Where the police know that a UNHCR staff member may visit, or that following an initial visit the staff member will be returning, this may deter mistreatment. Such visits are also reassuring to the detainee and may be used to enquire whether family members are aware of the detention.

Liaison with the International Committee of the Red Cross (ICRC), who have primary responsibility for detainees, is important.

k) Family reunification
- Ensure, where desired, reunification of families separated in different camps or inside the same camp, as well as between the country of origin, the country of asylum, and the country of resettlement so as to reduce the number of unaccompanied vulnerable individuals.

l) Screening and monitoring of unaccompanied children in foster care
- Where unaccompanied children are placed in foster families, the foster family should be properly screened before placement. Close monitoring should follow placement to ensure the welfare of the child, and in particular that the child is not sexually abused by members of the foster family.

m) Personal documentation

Urges States, relevant United Nations organizations, as well as non-governmental organizations, as appropriate, to...

Issue individual identification and/or registration documents to all refugee women;...

Executive Committee Conclusion No. 64 (XLI) (1990), paragraph (a) (viii)
Refugee Women and International Protection

Calls upon States and UNHCR to ensure the equal access of women and men to all forms of personal documentation relevant to refugees' freedom of movement, welfare and civil status...

Executive Committee Conclusion No. 73 (XLIV) (1993), paragraph (c)
Refugee Protection and Sexual Violence

- Ensure that refugee women have proper personal documentation and access on an equal basis with men to whatever registration process is used to determine eligibility for assistance.

n) Choice of assistance and/or resources

- Ensure that the choice of assistance and/or resources does not expose individuals to greater risk (e.g. when collecting firewood in isolated areas is dangerous, try to provide alternative forms of fuel, provide energy-efficient stoves, and/or change the food basket, in careful consultation with nutritionists and other experts, to foods that require less cooking time).

o) Fair distribution of food and non-food items

- Ensure that all essential items, such as food, water, shelter materials and firewood reach women by distributing the items to women directly, and/or by distribution administered by women.

p) Access to female protection and medical staff and female interpreters

Reiterates the importance of ensuring the presence of female field staff in refugee programmes, including emergency operations, and the direct access of refugee women to them;

Executive Committee Conclusion No. 73 (XLIV) (1993), paragraph (h)
Refugee Protection and Sexual Violence

- Ensure that refugee women have ready access to female protection staff and female interpreters, as well as to reproductive health facilities including female medical staff and gynecologists.

q) Establish fora for discussion and dispute resolution

- Establishing fora whereby refugees can air tensions and feuds which may have arisen between various groups or clans is important to prevent the build-up of hostile emotions which could later be manifested by acts of sexual violence.

r) Sensitization of local communities

- Providing information to the local community of the host country to give them an understanding of the refugees' situation can be important in reducing friction or tension between the two communities.
- Instigating channels of communication between refugees and the local community whereby disputes and complaints can be vented may help to prevent the build-up of tension and ill-feelings.

s) Assistance to local communities

- Assistance towards community development, such as improving local schools, airstrips or government facilities, can be instrumental in keeping the peace between the refugees and the host population. This may be particularly crucial when the arrival and presence of refugees have caused negative consequences to the local people, such as degradation of the environment and depletion of natural resources.

t) Combat frustration and boredom of male refugees

- Recognize the immense frustration, boredom and feeling of dependency which may be generated by camp life, and the relevance to physical security of developing channels for this energy, including through skills training, educational, recreational and income generating activities for males, particularly among the "long stayers" and adolescents.

u) Combat alcohol and drug abuse

- Organize an education campaign on the effects of alcohol abuse, using, inter alia, community structures, schools and/or posters.
- Provide counselling to alcohol and/or substance abusers, and those closely connected with them.
- Encourage involvement in activities of collective interest, such as educational and vocational training programmes, income generating activities and cultural and sporting activities.
- In refugee camps, stop illegal wire-tapping of electricity where it is used to supply alcohol-producing equipment.
- In refugee camps, in liaison with the authorities, consider placing limits on the consumption of alcohol.

2.2 Preventive Measures involving Human Resources Management

If the deterrent measures set out above are implemented, efforts to prevent sexual violence are a relatively inexpensive exercise relying on the cost-effective and equitable distribution of goods and services, the development or reinforcement of existing protection mechanisms, and most importantly, the involvement of the refugee community itself in providing protection to its members. The following preventive steps involve recruitment and deployment of staff.

a) Recruitment of female staff

- Ensure a gender balance among recruitment of professional staff at all levels by employing greater numbers of female protection officers, field interpreters, doctors, health workers and counsellors.

b) Presence of female protection officers

- Ensure in particular the presence of at least one well-trained female protection or field officer per field office, and more in areas where refugee women are known to have particular protection problems.
- Place trained international staff, including female staff, in key field locations such as areas which are major crossing points for refugees, reception centres, camps and returnee monitoring positions.

c) Visibility in the field

- UNHCR protection and field staff should make themselves visible in the field and meet with refugee women regularly to gain first-hand information on protection problems. Their presence and interest may provide a sense of security and reassurance among the female population and thus encourage them to speak up and seek assistance when their rights are violated.
- In areas where there are no principal crossing points, or in less frequented border areas, roving protection/field officers should be deployed.

d) Close links with traditional birth attendants

- Female medical and/or protection staff should establish and maintain close links with traditional birth attendants and other refugee health workers, who can be a valuable source of information on the incidence of sexual violence as well as providing a channel for disseminating relevant information to women in the

2.3 Preventive Measures involving the Host Government

Refugee workers and their organizations should stress to the authorities their duty to investigate, prosecute and punish perpetrators of sexual violence.

Urges States to respect and ensure the fundamental right of all individuals within their territory to personal security, inter alia by enforcing relevant national laws in compliance with international legal standards and by adopting concrete measures to prevent and combat sexual violence, including

(i) the development and implementation of training programmes aimed at promoting respect by law enforcement officers and members of military forces of the right of every individual, at all times and under all circumstances, to security of person, including protection from sexual violence,

(ii) implementation of effective, non-discriminatory legal remedies including the facilitation of the filing and investigation of complaints against sexual abuse, the prosecution of offenders, and timely and proportional disciplinary action in cases of abuse of power resulting in sexual violence,

(iii)arrangements facilitating prompt and unhindered access to all asylum seekers, refugees and returnees for UNHCR and, as appropriate, other organizations approved by the Governments concerned, and

(iv)activities aimed at promoting the rights of refugee women, including through the dissemination of the Guidelines on the Protection of Refugee Women and their implementation, in close cooperation with refugee women, in all sectors of refugee programmes;...

Executive Committee Conclusion No. 73 (XLIV) (1993), paragraph (b)
Refugee Protection and Sexual Violence

States should be urged to adopt a firm and highly visible policy against all forms of sexual violence û including those committed by government employees by taking the following steps:

a) Advocate enactment and enforcement of national legislation
- Advocate the enactment and/or enforcement of national laws against sexual violence in accordance with international legal standards. This will include prosecution of offenders and the implementation of legal measures for the protection of the victim, e.g. restraining orders.
- Ensure that Government policy does not exclude the applicability of national legislation to refugee camps.
- Promote the ratification of relevant international human rights instruments. Details of international legal obligations can be found in Chapter 4.

b) Liaison with national women's organizations
- National women's organizations in host countries can play a valuable role in advocating and addressing the issue of violence against women. Contacts can be established with them and discussions initiated regarding the role they can play. These can also be extended to include national health, lawyers and human rights associations.

c) Facilitate the investigation of complaints of sexual violence

- The provision of victim/witness advocate programmes could be used to assist victims. It involves one person being assigned to assist a victim as her case is processed, providing support and information about the process and education to family members if needed. This concept enhances the likelihood that cases actually proceed to court and can help to prevent the retraumatization of victims by the court system.

d) Ensure protection of the victim and any witnesses from reprisals

- Ensuring protection depends on the circumstances of the attack and must be assessed on a case-by-case basis. Factors to be taken into account include whether the perpetrator(s) are known to her, and whether the perpetrator(s) are able to locate her. For instance, an attack taking place in a refugee's home may be quite different from one which involves a group of women being attacked in the bush surrounding a camp. An assessment is necessary as to whether the victim was individually targeted or the attack happened at random.
- In a refugee camp situation this may entail the need to evacuate persons to another location.

e) Disciplinary action taken in cases involving government officials and refugee workers

- Advocate that prompt disciplinary action be taken in cases of abuse of power, corruption and lack of discipline of officials and refugee workers resulting in sexual violence.

f) Documentation and analysis of information

- Document cases to the extent necessary so that information can be used in assessing causes of sexual violence to assist the development of preventive and remedial strategies. Respect confidentiality to ensure the safety of refugees.

g) Sufficient presence of security personnel

- Ensure that an adequate number of security personnel, police and/or military, are present in refugee camps to provide physical protection from attackers. The number and the type of security personnel required will depend on a variety of factors, including the current security situation and the ability and performance of the existing forces in coping with that situation. Requests can be made both at the camp level and at a higher level by the UNHCR Branch Office to relevant government officials.

h) Deployment of female security personnel

- Where appropriate, deploy females as part of security forces or guards to encourage refugee women to report sexual violence incidents and to seek protection.

i) UNHCR support to national security forces where needed

- Ensure the early provision of logistical and communications support to national security forces where needed. Sometimes UNHCR may need to provide support by way of vehicles, fuel, or communications equipment to the host Government.

2.4 Preventive Measures involving Information, Education and Training

Supports the High Commissioner's efforts, in coordination with other intergovernmental and non-governmental organizations competent in this area, to develop and organize training courses for authorities, including camp officials, eligibility officers, and others dealing with refugees on practical protection measures for preventing and responding to sexual violence;...

Encourages the High Commissioner to pursue actively her efforts, in cooperation with bodies and organizations dealing with human rights, to increase awareness of the rights of refugees and the specific needs and abilities of refugee women and girls and to promote the full and effective implementation of the Guidelines on the Protection of Refugee Women;

Executive Committee Conclusion No. 73 (XLIV) (1993), paragraphs (i) and (k) Refugee Protection and Sexual Violence

a) Public information campaigns

Information campaigns are an important tool in combatting sexual violence. Public information campaigns should be launched on the issue of sexual violence, taking into account cultural sensitivities, ethics, and the particular circumstances prevailing in the country concerned.

Target groups for information activities could include:
- refugees
- UNHCR staff

- NGO staff
- government officials
- security personnel, including police officers and the military
- any others who come into contact with refugees.

Topics covered could include:
- preventive measures
- how and where to seek assistance if sexually attacked
- national and international laws prohibiting sexual violence
- sanctions and penalties associated with acts of sexual violence.

Tools which could be utilized in such campaigns include:
- pamphlets, newsletters, information bulletins, posters
- community entertainment (songs, theatre)
- verbal presentations at public or community meetings
- NGO networks, religious or other groups
- radio and other mass media
- videos.

The assistance of NGOs and refugees, particularly female refugees, may be sought in developing appropriate training programmes. Video education in public information campaigns may be particularly effective. Preparing and disseminating statistics on sexual violence in refugee situations may help others become aware of this problem.

Correct false rumours and misinformation
If it becomes known that false rumours are circulating in the refugee camps in relation to sexual violence, an immediate information campaign should be launched to dispel them. (An example might be the rumour that "rape victims will receive cash benefits or resettlement opportunities").

b) Training courses could focus on:
- how to prevent sexual violence and how to respond to incidents of sexual violence (immediate and long-term action and follow-up) using these Guidelines;
- the causes and consequences of sexual violence;
- legal awareness;

- basic human rights and responsibilities. The UNHCR Training Module *Human Rights and Refugee Protection*,1995, is available as training material;
- the rights to personal security under national and international law, with a particular emphasis on the rights of women and girls;
- interviewing skills. The UNHCR Training Module *Interviewing Applicants for Refugee Status*, 1995, is available as training material.

c) In addition, various groups may benefit from more specialized training in specific areas, for example:

Refugees and local communities

Refugees and local communities should be provided with education and training, presented in a culturally appropriate way, preferably created with the involvement of refugee women.

Objectives include:
- modifying negative attitudes towards the victims of sexual violence;
- reinforcing and fostering concepts of community responsibility for protecting and assisting its vulnerable members and assisting their families.

Suggestions include:
- educating the refugees as to their responsibilities under the laws of the country of asylum and in particular the penalties associated with violence, including sexual violence;
- widely disseminating information about cases resulting in conviction, and the sentence administered;
- informing the refugee population and the local population that UNHCR and the international community take a strong position against sexual violence. Ways suggested above under (a) Public information campaigns could be used.

Recognize the influence of community and religious leaders in this context and enlist their cooperation in changing attitudes towards sexual violence, both in terms of prevention and in alleviating the effect on the victims.

Refugee women

Female refugees should be made aware of their legal rights and responsibilities. In particular, they should be made aware of the Universal

Declaration of Human Rights, the Convention on the Elimination of All Forms of Discrimination against, Women, the Convention on the Rights of the Child and the Declaration on the Elimination of Violence against Women.

Urges the High Commissioner to undertake initiatives for refugee women in the areas of leadership and skills training, legal awareness, and education; and in particular in the area of reproductive health, with full respect for the various religious and ethical values and cultural backgrounds of the refugees, in conformity with universally recognized international human rights and the UNHCR Guidelines on the Protection of Refugee Women.

Executive Committee Conclusions on the Recommendation of the Working Group: Refugee Women (1994), paragraph (b)

It is important that refugee women know in advance about the facilities and forms of assistance which are available to them should they be sexually attacked so that they can avail themselves of this help.

Refugee women should know that confidentiality will be respected and that they will be treated with sensitivity and compassion. Victims should be made comfortable about coming forward. This sort of information may encourage reporting of incidents and thereby increase the provision of assistance and protection to victims.

In particular, refugee women should be informed in advance of "do's" and "don'ts", for example:
- the need to have a medical examination as early as possible following a sexual , attack;
- to avoid washing themselves immediately following an attack as this will affect the results of any medical examination which may be crucial to any later criminal prosecution;
- to keep any evidence intact, such as preserving the clothes worn at the time of the incident without cleaning them.

Refugee leaders

Refugee leaders could be trained so that they will be in a better position to assist in modifying negative attitudes towards the victims and in fostering concepts of community responsibility. Moreover, such training could facilitate the dissemination of information on sexual violence and measures for prevention.

UNHCR, other concerned UN staff, and NGO staff

UNHCR, other concerned UN staff, and NGO staff should be aware of their duty to uphold and implement UNHCR policy as contained in the Policy on Refugee Women, the Guidelines on the Protection of Refugee Women, the Policy on Refugee Children and the Guidelines on Refugee Children, as well as these Guidelines. They should furthermore be aware of UNHCR Executive Committee Conclusions touching on this issue (in particular those relating to refugee women and sexual violence).

All UN staff members, including members of peace-keeping forces, should be reminded of their obligation to ensure that their activities conform to norms established in United Nations human rights instruments, including the Universal Declaration of Human Rights, the Convention on the Elimination of All Forms of Discrimination against Women, the Convention on the Rights of the Child and the Declaration on the Elimination of Violence against Women.

UNHCR staff, particularly field and protection officers and interpreters, should be well-trained in interviewing skills and how to deal with incidents of sexual violence. NGO staff should be aware of their role in preventing and responding to sexual violence. These Guidelines and the Guidelines on the Protection of Refugee Women can be used as basic documents.

Government officials

Government officials should be informed of their responsibility and of the measures they should take to protect the rights of refugees, with particular emphasis on the national laws and the relevant international human rights instruments that they have ratified, and UNHCR'sExecutive Committee Conclusion No. 73 (XLIV) (1993) on Refugee Protection and Sexual Violence (contained in Annex 4).

Members of the security forces

Members of the security forces should be advised of the relevant codes of conduct aimed at preventing and redressing abuse of power, in particular that which involves the commission of acts of sexual violence. They should be made aware of the problem of sexual violence and ways of taking preventive and remedial protective action. Furthermore, they should be trained in interviewing skills and how to support the needs of victims to enable them to handle these cases appropriately.

d) Role of the media and human rights reports

The media and human rights reports can play an important role in some situations by putting pressure on States to provide physical protection to refugees.

See 5.1 Dealing with the Media.

2.5 Preventive Measures in the Context of Voluntary Repatriation

Calls upon States and UNHCR... to encourage the participation of refugee women as well as men in decisions relating to their voluntary repatriation or other durable solutions;

Executive Committee Conclusion No. 73 (XLIV) (1993), paragraph (c)
Refugee Protection and Sexual Violence

UNHCR voluntary repatriation programmes should attempt to combat the problem of sexual violence by taking the following steps:

- Promote and implement family reunification in the pre-repatriation stage.
- Ensure that families, including extended families, can travel as a unit. The same applies for groups of refugees, who have developed a social network in the camp (e.g. groups of female-headed households and unaccompanied women) who wish to return to the same destination. This could be ensured by linking together voluntary repatriation forms for joint travel.
- Ensure that refugee women, on an equal basis with refugee men, are provided with a viable opportunity to declare individually their desire to return or opt out of a voluntary repatriation, and have equal access to information on which to base their decision.
- Ensure the physical safety of areas, such as reception centres and transit camps and their facilities, by adopting relevant measures suggested under Design and location of refugee camps in 2.1(a) above.
- Ensure that protection activities focused on returnees give high priority to assessing the safety of returnee women. Special attention should be paid to especially vulnerable individuals, for example the disabled, pregnant women and unaccompanied minors, by identifying them early in repatriation planning and developing specific procedures to transport and receive them.
- Ensure that protection and field officers monitoring the return have a thorough knowledge of the UNHCR Guidelines on the Protection of Refugee Women and these Guidelines.

CHAPTER 3: PRACTICAL GUIDELINES ON RESPONDING TO INCIDENTS OF SEXUAL VIOLENCE

Each incident of sexual violence must be examined and assessed for the required action in each of the following areas:
1. Protection
2. Medical
3. Psychosocial

KEY POINTS TO REMEMBER

- Ensure the physical safety of the victim.
- Prevent any further suffering by the victim
- Be guided by the best interests of the victim.
- Respect the victim's wishes in all instances.
- Guarantee confidentiality.

Strict confidentiality is essential. Wherever possible a victim's anonymity should be maintained. Written information on the victim must be kept locked and secure from others.

If confidentiality is breached it could bring grave consequences for the victim, particularly if adequate protection is not in place. It may discourage others from coming forward.

- Be sensitive, discreet, friendly and compassionate when dealing with the victim.
- Ensure same-gender interviewer/interpreter/doctor.

Recommends that refugee victims of sexual violence and their families be provided with adequate medical and psychosocial care, including culturally appropriate counselling facilities, and generally be considered as persons of special concern to States and to UNHCR with respect to assistance and the search for durable solutions;

Executive Committee Conclusion No. 73 (XLIV) (1993), paragraph (f)
Refugee Protection and Sexual Violence

3.1 General

Acts of sexual violence violate basic human rights. Therefore, UNHCR staff have an obligation to intervene whenever cases are reported or suspected. The immediate physical and emotional consequences of sexual violence require a quick response. However, careful handling is required due to the extreme sensitivity of sexual issues in general and of sexual violence in particular. It is important to try to provide an environment in which refugees feel they can report protection problems privately, secure in the knowledge that there will be no retribution, and that confidentiality will be assured. The victim's immediate or long-term vulnerability must be taken into consideration, and the victim's own decisions must be respected.

Problem of association

Experience has shown that a "problem of association" may result if one specific person is tasked to work only with victims of sexual violence. Anyone coming to see this person might be branded as a "rape victim" and be stigmatized. Staff should take every precaution not to draw attention to women who have been subjected to sexual violence. Similarly, separate projects for such women should be avoided.

The link of UNHCR staff and medical personnel

It is important that the community services officers, protection officers, field officers, resettlement officers and medical personnel work together as a team.

UNHCR staff dealing with a victim of sexual violence are encouraged to share their interview notes with each other in order to make a second interview unnecessary. No more information about the incident than absolutely necessary should be sought (see Obtaining relevant information in 3.4 below).

3.2 The Rights of the Accused

Where the accused is a refugee, UNHCR has a responsibility towards him also.

Fair trial and humane treatment

The accused is entitled to be treated with the rights accorded to a person whose guilt is not proven. UNHCR has an obligation to him to ensure that he has a fair trial and is subjected to humane treatment in the course of interrogation and incarceration.

Terminology

Until such time as a court of law has found an accused guilty of the sexual violence for which he is charged, the accused should be properly referred to as the "alleged perpetrator" or the "accused", rather than as "the rapist" and the like.

3.3 Identifying Incidents of Sexual Violence

- One of the most effective ways of "tapping" the refugee information network to identify cases of sexual violence is to facilitate the establishment of women's groups and associations, thereby giving individual women a channel to report attacks. Experience has shown that an effective mechanism is a women's health clinic which deals with women's physical health, and thus offers a "safe" environment for revealing attacks. (However, care should be taken not to set up such groups merely as "cover" for detecting sexual violence). Other groups could be in relation to recreational, leisure or income-generating activities. These groups have significant additional benefits such as providing a network for communication and information flow and a structure for community support in the aftermath of sexual violence, as well as reinforcing preventive action.
- Keep close contact with community members and leaders to discover whether a young girl or woman is being held in isolation or whether people talk about her in a disapproving way. This might indicate that she is a victim of sexual violence. In the case of male victims, the taboos are so strong that it is extremely unlikely that an incident will be revealed or acknowledged even to this limited extent.
- Look for signs of trauma, such as reports of pains, nightmares, loss of appetite, headaches, sadness, fear, confusion, loss of memory, attention problems, isolation and talk of suicide.
- Discreetly look for signs of physical violence.
- Collect and study background materials and refugee stories describing the circumstances of flight. Such information can indicate situations where sexual violence is likely to occur or has occurred.

Where Sexual Violence is Suspected but the Person is Reluctant to Discuss
- Where sexual violence is suspected but the person is reluctant to report the incident, it is advisable for a social worker, health worker, community services officer or protection officer to meet privately with the suspected victim either alone or with a trusted person of her choice. In such a

situation it is vital that the officer, and any interpreter, be of the same gender as the person. However, there may be cases where a person requests to speak to someone of the opposite gender, e.g. male victims may prefer discussing sexual violence with females.

- There is no hard and fast rule for dealing with situations where sexual violence is suspected to have occurred but the person is unwilling to discuss the issue. Staff dealing with this should take a very delicate approach, being extremely careful not to push the person. Being forceful with the individual may cause retraumatization and further suffering.
- If the family is sympathetic towards the suspected victim, and where it is culturally appropriate to do so, it may be helpful to meet with the family to find out whether they have noticed a problem and give advice on how to handle it.

3.4 Steps to Take in Response

a) General

Once an incident of sexual violence has been revealed the following steps should be taken:

- Staff handling the victim of sexual violence must always be sympathetic yet professional. The victim should immediately be provided with privacy and be reassured about her safety. She should not be pressured to talk nor be left alone for long periods.

Medical treatment

- If the incident has occurred recently, the victim may require immediate medical care and should be escorted to the appropriate medical facilities. Post-coital contraception may be available to prevent a rape victim from becoming pregnant.

See 3.8 Medical Response below.

Contacting the police

- In addition, it may be necessary to contact the police immediately, if the victim so decides, in order that they investigate the case, particularly where there is the possibility of apprehending the perpetrator(s). The victim should be advised as to the likely course of events following police notification in order to make her decision about whether the authorities should be contacted.

See chapter 4 on Legal Aspects.

Obtaining relevant information

The staff member should seek no more information about the incident than absolutely necessary to establish what took place, where, and by whom.

- When an interview is possible, and with the consent of the victim, relevant information should be obtained about the-circumstances of the incident details about the victim, the perpetrator(s); when the incident(s) occurred; where, and who, if anyone, witnessed the occurrence. See the sample sexual violence information form in Annex 2.
- The focus should be on trying to clarify the circumstances sufficiently to determine what, if any, further action should be taken. It is not a test of the victim's credibility nor should it be seen as an opportunity for building a court case against the alleged offender.
- Staff should strive to ensure that only one interview is conducted to establish the events.

See 3.6 Conducting an Interview below.

Same gender and continuity of staff involvement

- A trained staff member of the same gender must always conduct related interviews with the victim, unless the victim requests otherwise. The same staff member(s) should remain involved in the case throughout to avoid the victim being handed from one person to another and having to repeat the same painful information.

Exchange of information

- With full respect for confidentiality, UNHCR staff (field officers, protection officers, community services officers, resettlement officers) should exchange information available on cases in order to avoid retraumatizing the victim by obliging her to repeat her story.

Confidentiality

- The information must be treated as strictly confidential, unless the victim decides otherwise.

Follow-up action

- At the conclusion of the first or subsequent interview, the interviewer should determine whether the victim requires (further) medical help, legal advice and/or counselling, and make the necessary referrals.

Ensure physical safety of victim
- If the victim's living situation is unsafe, measures should be taken to ensure safety. This may include those such as removal to a safe house or an emergency room, or immediate transfer from a camp, while ensuring at all times the victim's privacy.
- If the victim is unaccompanied, it may also be helpful to house her with female friends to support and assist her during this critical time.

Where the alleged perpetrator is a member of the police or military, or another government officer
- Immediate measures are necessary where the alleged perpetrators are amongst those who are responsible for the safety of the refugees, e.g. the police guarding a refugee camp.
- Depending on the wishes of the victim, immediate measures may involve bringing the incident to the attention of high level government officials by convening a meeting to present the allegations and decide on an appropriate course of action. It may also be useful to give the government officials at the meeting, or subsequent to it, a letter written by UNHCR outlining the allegations and UNHCR's expectation of a speedy and thorough investigation. It may be particularly useful to forward a copy of the correspondence to superiors of the local officials, e.g., where refugee camps are in remote areas and there is a general breakdown of law and order, or a lack of discipline among the security personnel.
- Where appropriate, an identification parade should be arranged as soon as possible through the highest local authorities/police/military officials present. In such circumstances extreme caution should be taken to ensure the safety and protection of the victim and any refugee witnesses. For instance, in some situations, if the alleged sexual violence occurred in a refugee camp it may be necessary to evacuate the victim, refugee witnesses and any accompanying family members as soon as possible, with interim protection measures being made.
- Punishment of one official for sexual violence may deter others in authority from committing further acts.

Replacement of clothes and non-food items
- It may be necessary to replace the victim's clothes so that she does not wear those worn during the attack. If essential non-food items belonging to the victim, such as shelter or blankets, were looted, these should be

replaced immediately upon verification. The community service workers may be able to perform the necessary verification.

- Where clothes are replaced, care must be taken so that women cannot be identified as victims of sexual violence by particular clothing characteristics (e.g., do not give victims cloth of the same fabric).

Legal Action
- It is up to the victim to decide about criminal prosecution or the initiation of a civil suit, depending on the legal system. The victim should be advised of all relevant information, including possible consequences, before she makes the decision whether to bring the incident to the attention of the authorities. UNHCR, NGO or adequate legal support should be available throughout any court procedures if the victim so desires.

See 4.1 National Law.

Possible Resettlement
- Depending on the security situation and the victim's mental and û physical condition, consideration may be given to resettlement on emergency or nonemergency grounds. It is emphasized that resettlement is rarely a "solution" under these circumstances.

b) Specific Situations

i) Where sexual violence has resulted in pregnancy (and termination of pregnancy is medically viable).

See 3.8 Medical Response.

ii) Where sexual violence has resulted in pregnancy and the victim is unable or unwilling to legally terminate the pregnancy or the situation does not come to the attention of staff until it is too late to terminate the pregnancy.
- All options, e.g., keeping the child, foster care and adoption, should be discussed with the woman concerned, regardless of the individual beliefs of the counsellors, medical staff or other involved persons, in order to enable the woman to make an informed decision at a later stage.
- Close medical monitoring is necessary.
- Counselling and support are essential.

iii) Children Born as a Result of Rape

Children who are born as a result of rape may be mistreated, or even abandoned by their mothers and families. These children may become malnourished and may lack the necessary care and attention.

This is an extremely sensitive area with no simple answers. However, the following points are stressed:

- The situation will require very close monitoring.
- Extreme care must be taken not to stigmatize the mother or the child.
- The situation should be dealt with to the extent possible by the ordinary community support structures and existing systems of child welfare.
- Additional support to the mother, in relation to assistance and psychological help, may be needed.
- The welfare of the child may warrant consideration of options such as foster placement and, later, adoption. A cautious approach should be taken.

3.5 Sexual Violence in Domestic Situations

There are no easy responses to sexual violence against refugees when it is committed in a domestic environment. The following general guidance is provided based on a common sense approach that should be borne in mind at all times.

Extreme caution should be exercised before any intervention is made. Concerned staff should be aware of the possible difficulties that may arise following intervention. In some situations, more harm may be caused to the victim and other relatives by becoming involved than had the matter been left alone.

Awareness of repercussions and limits of UNHCR intervention

- While intentions may be good, give careful forethought to the possible repercussions of any proposed action.
- Be attentive to the fact that the victim may decide to return, or may have no alternative but to return, to reside with the abuser at the end of the day.
- Retaliation against the victim or relatives may result if the abuser learns that the victim or other family members have brought the incident to the attention of others.
- UNHCR staff should be aware of the limits of the action able to be taken by the Office in this context.

Careful Assessment
- Before any intervention is made each situation must be carefully assessed on an individual basis with due regard to the particular cultural context.

Close Liaison with Colleagues
- Before taking any action discuss possible approaches with relevant colleagues, such as the field officer, protection officer and community services officer, in order to benefit from their expertise, share strategies and points of view. They may also have additional information on the case which is not known by you.
- Following a careful assessment, and where intervention is determined as the most appropriate response, it may be useful for colleagues to act together, such as, for example, the protection officer teaming up with the community services officer.

Possible Interventions
- One approach may be to identify the possible root causes of the aggression and examine ways to redress them.
- Where appropriate, refer the matter to a disciplinary committee or other mechanism in place or, if the offence is of sufficient gravity, the authorities may have to be contacted.

Suspected Domestic Violence
- Where sexual violence is suspected in domestic situations, very discreet advice to the suspected victim on any options available to her may be appropriate.

Possible types of action to be taken in advance:
- Inform refugees of different forms of assistance that may be available to persons subjected to domestic violence (e.g., counselling services, options for safe alternative accommodation).
- Educate refugees as to their basic human rights as defined by international norms. See 2.4 Preventive Measures Involving Information, Education and Training and 4.2 International Law for more detail.

Children
- Where domestic sexual abuse of refugee children is involved, intervention may be crucial to ensure their physical and psychosocial well-being.

Remember that children are more vulnerable than adults on whom they depend for protection.

"[UNHCR] must act when the safety and liberty of refugee children is at risk, either directly or indirectly".
UNHCR Guidelines on Refugee Children at page 81.

For additional information, refer to UNHCR Guidelines on Refugee Children, chapter 4 on "Psychosocial Well-being" and chapter 7 on "Personal Liberty and Security".

3.6 Conducting an Interview

Where the victim is unable or unwilling to discuss the incident
- If the victim is unable or unwilling to discuss the matter, the staff member should ask discreet and indirect questions. If she is still unwilling to share her problem, the staff member should not force the issue, but assure the person that staff are always available to assist her once she is ready to talk about the problem. She should not be left alone but a close relative or friend should be found to keep an eye on her.

Children
- If the victim is under the age of majority of the host country (commonly 18 years) then the consent of his or her parents or legal guardian should first be obtained. A child may feel more comfortable being interviewed in the presence of his or her parent, another family member or a trusted adult. The child should be consulted on this.
- Where a child is involved, interviewing techniques should be adopted accordingly, using simpler language, spending more time establishing rapport with the child and developing a trusting relationship. In addition, if an interpreter is being used he or she should be specifically trained to work with children, e.g., a child welfare worker, or a teacher.

See also the sections on "Interviewing Skills" and "Preparing and Conducting an Interview" on pages 28-39 of the UNHCR Manual Working with Unaccompanied Minors in the Community.

Opening the interview
- The first step should be to establish a basic rapport with the victim. The interviewer should take the time to introduce him/herself and the interpreter, explain clearly what his or her role is and the exact purpose of the interview.
- The victim should be informed that she does not have to be interviewed, can refuse to answer any questions that she does not feel comfortable with, and can stop the interview at any time.

Confidentiality
- The victim should be assured of confidentiality vis-a-vis her immediate family, the extended family, the refugee community, and, where requested by her, the camp authorities and police. Confidentiality can be TOTAL if the victim insists that nothing should be done.

Demeanour of interviewer
- It is essential that the interviewer remain neutral, compassionate, sensitive and objective during the interview.

Recording information
- With an assurance of absolute confidentiality, notes should be taken contemporaneously and in a discreet manner. The individual should know that the conversation is being documented. Post facto notes are likely to be erroneous.

Irrelevance of previous sexual history except in relation to past sexual attacks

The previous sexual history of a victim is irrelevant for UNHCR interviewing purposes and should not be asked of the victim, except in relation to any previous sexual attacks.

Knowledge of any previous sexual (or other) attacks is relevant to both protection of the victim and her psychosocial well-being. Regarding protection, knowledge of a previous attack may suggest that the victim has been specifically targeted rather than chosen at random and may thus need more urgent and drastic protection measures to be taken. Regarding her psychosocial well-being, an individual who has already experienced sexual violence may be more psychologically vulnerable and more prone to retraumatization requiring additional efforts and sensitivity.

Retraumatization
- The interviewer should be extremely careful not to cause retraumatization. This occurs when a "triggering" event causes the victim to be overwhelmed by memory and feelings from the previous trauma. As such, questioning should be done gently and discreetly and at the victim's own pace. On no account should she be pressured to speak if she is unwilling to do so. (See Retraumatization in 3.9 for more detail).

Shock or psychic numbing
- Remember that a victim may at the time of the interview be experiencing shock or psychic numbing due to trauma with the consequence that her emotions are significantly muted. (See "Psychic Numbing" in 3.9 for more detail).

Where an interpreter is being used
- The interpreter should be the same gender as the victim.
- The interviewer and the interpreter should be aware of difficulties in interpreting. For example, words such as "rape" or "assault" may have different meanings or connotations in the victim's language.
- As with all other interviews involving an interpreter, the interviewer should ask all questions directly to the interviewee. Recall at all times that the primary role of the interpreter is to facilitate communication, and in no way should the interpreter control or direct the interview.

Concluding an interview
- At the conclusion of the interview, the victim should be reassured of her safety, and any follow-up action explained. She should also be given the opportunity to ask any questions.

Some additional practical tips:

Interview setting
- The place of interview should be in a confidential and quiet setting, one which makes the victim feel comfortable, safe and at ease and one that would not lead others to assume that she is a rape victim. In a camp, this could be at the UNHCR offices, at offices where eligibility interviews take place, or a room at the hospital. Care should be taken not to draw attention to the person being interviewed.

No interruptions
- Avoid any interruptions or distractions during the interview, such as telephone calls or others coming into the office during that time. In the same way, switch off any walkie-talkies, unless they are crucial for security purposes.

Be prepared
- Have drinking water and some tissues at hand.

For more detail refer to the UNHCR Training Module Interviewing Applicants for Refugee Status.

3.7 Reporting Requirements

Situation Reports
- General reporting on the situation of sexual violence against refugees should be done from each field office to the head UNHCR office in each country. This is usually through the weekly situation reports ("sitreps"). It is also expected that this information will form part of the regular sitreps from each head UNHCR office in the field to Headquarters.

Particularly Serious Cases
- As with any protection problem, UNHCR Headquarters intervention can be sought on cases of a particularly serious nature. Advice can also be requested from Headquarters on any case.

3.8 Medical Response

Same-gender medical personnel
- A doctor (or a health worker if a doctor is not available) of the same gender as the victim should always conduct the initial medical examination(s) and follow-up. This is considered essential for cultural, psychological and security reasons. In many cultures it is taboo or extremely embarrassing for a person to be touched or examined by a doctor of the opposite gender. This is particularly so in the case of women and could significantly add to the trauma which has already been experienced. In such instances, examination by a male doctor would be perceived as highly distressing and even threatening and is therefore to be avoided. If however, there is no option, the situation should be discussed with the victim and she should be prepared for a referral to a male doctor.

Local doctors to conduct medical examination where possible
- In refugee camps, medical practitioners from the host country, rather than international doctors, should conduct examinations and write medical reports since they will be in a better position to give evidence in any later legal proceedings if they occur. For example, by the time the case has reached the courts, a foreign doctor may have left the country and it may not be possible for him/her to return. In some situations, however, local doctors may not be prepared to testify if local agents are the alleged perpetrators.

Preparing the victim
- It is advisable that the victim be prepared for the physical examination which will follow since sometimes medical procedures themselves are traumatic. Therefore, the staff member must be familiar with the examination procedures, and be able to explain them to her in non-technical language.
- In certain situations it may be advisable for this staff member to accompany the victim to the examination.
- In-patient treatment or out-patient treatment may include: tests for sexually transmitted diseases (VDRL); analgesia; post-coital contraception; antibiotics; tetanus toxoid/immunoglobulin injection; blood investigations; hepatitis B tests.

The following medical procedures should be taken
- A counsellor, nurse or physician should document a detailed history of the attack including force or threats used, the nature of any penetration which took place, and whether ejaculation occurred. Essential elements also include whether the victim bathed, urinated, excreted or changed clothes following the attack; any symptoms following the assault, recent menstrual and contraceptive history.
- Obtaining information about the past sexual history is, generally, neither necessary nor relevant. The mental state of the individual should be assessed and noted.
- A medical examination should be made including documentation of the witnessed examination, condition of the clothing, any foreign material adhering to the body, any evidence of trauma however minor, and results of a pelvic examination. This clinical examination should entail a complete physical examination which should not begin immediately with the sexual sphere or be limited thereto.

- Observation of external signs, such as the condition of clothes and a collection of material which might serve as evidence should be made. Material which the medical staff might collect for evidence (where forensic pathology laboratories exist), includes plucked hair, fingernail scrapings, combing from the pubic area, clothing, fluid and swabs from the vaginal and/or anal vaults for sperm, saliva and blood samples. It is necessary to obtain the consent of the victim for the collection of such evidence and its conveyance to the law enforcement authorities.

Vulnerability of pregnant women
- Women who are pregnant at the time of the sexual violence are physically and psychologically more vulnerable. In particular, they are susceptible to miscarriages, hypertension and premature births.

Post-coital contraception ("Emergency Contraception")
- In countries where the "morning-after pill" (or "day-after pill"), or other forms of post-coital contraception, are legal and available, it should be offered to a rape victim, once its effects have been fully and carefully explained to her. Trauma can be reduced by preventing a rape victim from becoming pregnant.
- The "morning-after pill" can be effective up to 72 hours post-coitally; the sooner it is used, the more effective it is likely to be. This form of contraception prevents pregnancy by stimulating the process of early menstruation before egg implantation. According to the World Health Organization it does not constitute an abortion.

Increased risk of contracting HIV
- The tearing injuries and open wounds of the women's genital tract from force used in rape increases the risk of contracting HIV from an infected man.

High risk of STD transmission in situations of armed conflict
- Army recruits have been recognized as a category tending to show higher rates of STDs (sexually transmitted diseases) than the general population. In situations of rape during armed conflict a high risk of STD transmission should be assumed. Prophylactic therapy (i.e. without making a clinical diagnosis), using appropriate antibiotics, should be considered to cover the major treatable infections, particularly gonorrhoea, chlamydia and syphilis, that could otherwise have long-term consequences.

Vulnerability of girls to the effects of STDs
- Girls who have not completed puberty are particularly vulnerable to the effects of STDs because the lining of the genital tract has yet to take on its adult character. STDs contracted at this age entail a greater risk of permanent damage such as infertility or ectopic pregnancy (where pregnancy occurs in the Fallopian tube) later in life.

Risks of HIV and other STDs and pregnancy
- The individual should be advised of the risks of contracting HIV and STDs. The risk of pregnancy should be discussed with female victims. HIV and pregnancy tests should be offered.
- UNHCR and the World Health Organization have finalized guidelines in connection with HIV. These Guidelines for Early HIV Intervention in Emergency Settings should be referred to, particularly in relation to counselling and maintaining confidentiality.

Where sexual violence has resulted in pregnancy
- All options. e.g., keeping the child, adoption and abortion, should be discussed with the woman concerned, regardless of the individual beliefs of the counsellors, medical staff or other involved persons, in order to enable the woman to make an informed decision.
- It should be noted that in some countries abortion is illegal or is only permitted under limited circumstances. In some countries, for example, it may be necessary to obtain special permission from the authorities, or abortion may only be permitted for medical reasons. It is noted that in many countries abortion is legal in situations where a woman is pregnant as a result of rape. The counsellor must be aware of the legal situation with regard to abortion in the country of asylum or return, and this must be explained to the woman.
- Following comprehensive counselling, if the woman decides to terminate her pregnancy, this should be carried out under appropriate medical and psychological conditions.

See also 3.4 under b) Specific Situations.

Follow-up visits
- Follow-up visits should be arranged according to the necessity of each case. Repetition of HIV test should be offered in appropriate circumstances.

Strict confidentiality
- The importance of maintaining strict confidentiality is stressed.

3.9 Psychosocial Response

This section provides an overview of psychological reactions experienced by victims of sexual violence and action required to address their psychosocial needs.

Each person will experience and cope with the traumatic incident differently. See also 1.5 Effects of Sexual Violence.

a) Common Psychological Reactions
- The victim most commonly experiences fear, helplessness and humiliation. She is likely to experience a loss of trust and a loss of sense of safety and security.
- The victim will probably feel guilt or shame from a sense that perhaps she provoked or in some other way was responsible for what happened to her (also referred to as "classic rape syndrome").
- The victim's trauma may also lead to aggressiveness or destructiveness, anger, hatred or revenge, taking an outward direction instead of being internalized or assuming the blame.
- The experience of sexual violence often makes the victim feel unclean and unworthy. Virginity, modesty and female chastity define the value of girls and women in many cultures, and consequently sexual abuse is perceived as devaluing a woman and making her 'unclean'.
- Similarly. men are defined in many cultures in terms of their manhood and virility and therefore the experience of sexual violence against a man or boy can have a devastating psychological impact.
- "Psychic numbing":it is commonly thought that someone who has been sexually violated will be hysterical and cry uncontrollably, but in fact this is not the most common response. A victim can respond to sexual violence trauma by "psychic numbing". This is a defensive reaction that significantly mutes the person's emotions. She may feel numb, show little feeling, speak slowly and inaudibly and may appear very calm.

- Understanding this reaction is particularly important because that is how many victims appear during initial interviews and in their daily lives post-trauma. Victims of trauma commonly adopt strong defence mechanisms which include forgetting, denial and deep repression of the events during the immediate aftermath of the trauma, when the victim is still operating in "survival mode".

- After the initial shock and trauma of the incident, the victim might go through a period of thinking frequently about the incident, about the attacker, and re-experiencing the trauma. This may occur in connection with preparations for court proceedings or in preparation for eligibility interviews and will require careful monitoring and counselling.

- From the psychological point of view the reactions can range from minor depressions, grief, anxiety, phobia, somatic problems to serious and chronic mental conditions.

- Extreme reactions to sexual violence may result in suicide, or in the case of pregnancy, physical abandonment/elimination of the child.

- Retramautization: the concept of "retraumatization" is important to understand. This occurs when a "triggering" event causes the victim to be overwhelmed by memory and feelings from the previous trauma. It has been described as the psychological equivalent of having a scab torn off. It is painful, and can deplete what little emotional resources the victim has built up. The incident of sexual violence may in itself trigger retraumatization due to a previous trauma the person has experienced. Further, retraumatization may occur as a consequence of being interviewed in relation to a sexual attack.

b) Children

Children are more vulnerable to trauma and to retraumatization than adults. This is because children are developing. They grow in developmental sequences, each sequence depending on the one below it. Serious delays interrupting these sequences can severely disrupt development. All children are at developmental risk in situations of violent displacement, but sexual abuse, especially if it is ongoing, can have very harmful long-term psychological and psychosocial consequences.

The child as a direct victim

- The effects on a child resulting from personally suffering sexual violence will be mediated by age, gender and developmental level, and particularly by the capacity of the child's caregivers to give the child the necessary nurture and support.

- Who perpetrated the sexual attack will be a matter of significance: a stranger, a family member, and whether the abuse was ongoing or an isolated event. If there is an ongoing sexually exploitative relationship in a camp situation, for example, it would have very negative implications for the child's capacity to develop and maintain normal social relationships and age and gender appropriate behavior.

"Secondary" impact of sexual violence on a child
- A child may suffer as a result of sexual violence experienced by another person, most frequently the child's mother. Experiencing one traumatic event can compromise a mother's ability to care for her children. It may cause her to mediate the negative effects of sexual violence on her children's well-being and development. For example, in some cultures a woman may brake a number of cultural taboos if seen naked in front of her male children, or if they witness her engage in sexual activity. Should she be sexually attacked in front of her male children, her response may be to withdraw social and emotional contact from them as a result of her feelings of guilt and shame.

c) Care of Victims
   i) Children
   Every child has the right to "such protection and care as is necessary for his or her well-being".
   Every child who is a victim of "any form" of abuse or neglect has the right to "physical and psychological recovery and social reintegration".
The Convention of the Rights of the Child: Article 3(1) and Article 39.

   UNHCR staff are required to make their best efforts both to prevent risk to refugee children and to take additional action to ensure the survival and safety of refugee children at particular risk.
UNHCR Policy on Refugee Children, paragraph 26 (g).

   For specific guidance on how to help refugee children in relation to their psychosocial well-being, refer to Chapter 4: "Psychosocial Well-being" in UNHCR's Guidelines on Refugee Children (pages 37-51). This chapter explains why psychosocial well-being is important and contains guidance on how to help refugee children directly, by helping the family and by helping the community. The need for some children to receive specialized services or treatment due to having experienced damaging effects of trauma is dealt with on pages 48-49. Suggested age-appropriate activities for refugee children are also included.

ii) General

It is important to know what the response to sexual violence is according to the culture and traditions of the refugees. Victims should be treated with acceptance, care and support.

Support of family and friends
- In the long term, and in most cultural settings, the support of the victim's family and friends is likely to be the most important factor in overcoming the trauma of sexual violence. Efforts should therefore be made to encourage and maintain good relations with family and friends or to facilitate speedy family reunion where possible. For example, family and friends should be encouraged to accept a victim's apparent disorganization and/or uncustomary passivity and give support in managing daily activities and responsibilities. They may also need to provide help in making decisions.

Community support groups
- Efforts to relieve trauma suffering for the majority of cases are most appropriately handled through community-based activities which address psychosocial needs generally, rather than focusing specifically on sexual violence.
- It is important to encourage the establishment of community support groups which can counteract tendencies towards the social isolation of victims of sexual violence and problems in relation to friends, family members and the community. Clearly the form and approach of this kind of intervention will vary considerably according to the cultural context in which the violence has occurred. Where feasible, it can be helpful for such support groups to organize activities such as literacy, education, skills training, occupational therapy, music, sports, information, or any other useful daily activity.

Formal and informal women's groups
- Facilitating the establishment of formal and informal women's groups can provide an excellent framework for both preventive and therapeutic assistance. In most situations, keeping the victims active through recreational, psychosocial and/or income generating activities is very

effective psychological assistance. For example, women s groups or committees can provide a focus for establishing projects which promote useful activities, such as income generating projects, which can assist victims of sexual violence to regain control over some areas of their lives. Such activities can foster normalization of daily life and thereby contribute significantly to restoring or maintaining the mental health of refugee women, including those who have been sexually attacked.

Relocation of victim
- In some refugee camp situations, it may be helpful to discreetly transfer the victim and her family, if they desire, to another camp where refugees do not know about the incident. This may be necessary in situations where the victim would be ostracized by refugees who know about the incident.
- Where relocation occurs, extreme care and discretion should be used at the place of reception so that the transferees are not identified as being victims of sexual violence. Precautions to be taken will depend on the particular circumstances. It may also be necessary to inform the victim and any accompanying relatives not to divulge the real reason for the transfer.

d) Traumatic Effects on Family Members
- Sexual violence can have severe traumatic effects on the victim's family members or those friends who have witnessed the crime without being able to intervene, or who experience guilt for not having been present. This may be particularly the case for husbands who were present and were unable to prevent their wives from being raped, or for children who witnessed their mothers being sexually attacked.
- In such cases, individual and/or family counselling and close follow-up might be needed. In cases of family reunion where family members did not witness the incident, supportive counselling might be needed.

e) Counselling
Counselling should be provided only by trained mental health professionals. That is, a trained worker (such as a counsellor, nurse, social worker, psychologist, or psychiatrist), preferably from the same background as the victim.

In situations of continuing conflict it is particularly important to ensure that interviews with victims of sexual violence are conducted only by people with appropriate training and only if follow-up care by mental health professionals is available. Experience has shown that some women have attempted suicide after talking to the press and/or a "routine" interview with well-meaning information seekers. They need reassurance and total discretion.

Objectives of counselling
- help victims to understand what they have experienced and to develop a sense of control over their lives and to overcome their feelings of guilt;
- help victims to realize that they are not responsible for the attack, to stop blaming themselves and to understand that they are not alone, and that many other people have overcome such experiences and are leading normal lives;
- help victims to understand that feelings of anger, fear and guilt as well as unusual reactions and activities are common and natural; to encourage them to express anger towards their attacker(s) in order to alleviate feelings of self-blame;
- help in breaking the victim's social isolation and to ensure that they have access to support networks and services that meet their needs;
- help create an awareness in the community so that the victim can be provided with the necessary support, particularly within the family structure and within the larger community;
- help victims to remain or become active in daily activities.

Timely Counselling
In view of the potentially very serious and long lasting psychological effects of sexual violence, it is essential that the victim receive counselling as early as possible. Such immediate intervention can be very effective in minimizing the severity of psychological trauma in the longer term. On the other hand, if the incident remains unresolved, it may surface at any time in the future and can result in social dysfunction or, at worst, chronic mental disorder.

No Pressure
It is vital to ensure that the victim is ready for counselling. An individual who has experienced sexual violence should never be pressured into counselling as she may have built up psychological defences to deal with the experience. This is particularly important in situations of continuing conflict where the uncertainties of everyday existence may demand the maintenance of such defence mechanisms. It is also critical in situations where provision of ongoing counselling support is not ensured.

Counselling Personnel

Where possible, counsellors should work as part of a team with trained health and welfare workers of the same gender and culture as the victim. The counsellor and refugee workers should work closely with other service providers and members of the community, so that they are able to deal sympathetically and skillfully with victims of sexual violence

In some situations, where telephone services are available, the provision of a telephone counselling and referral service may be feasible and useful, particularly in locations where victims are widely dispersed.

For detailed information on appropriate therapeutic interventions, please refer to UNHCR *Guidelines on the Evaluation and Care of Victims of Trauma and Violence*. See also UNHCR *Community Services for Urban Refugees*, in particular pages 49-59 on "Victims of Violence".

Chapter 4: Legal Aspects Of Sexual Violence

This chapter discusses remedies under national law and practical steps to be taken having regard to national and international law The effect of sexual violence on the refugee status determination process is also examined.

4.1 National Law

The Government on whose territory the sexual attack has occurred is responsible for taking diligent remedial measures, including conducting a thorough investigation into the crime, identifying and prosecuting those responsible, and protecting victims from reprisals.

Advocacy of the Enactment and/or Enforcement of National Laws
UNHCR can help States to appreciate that serious, concerted action is needed in this regard. UNHCR should advocate the enactment and/or enforcement of national laws against sexual violence in accordance with international legal obligations. This will include prosecution of offenders and the implementation of legal measures for the protection of the victim (for example, restraining orders).

Awareness of the National Laws and Practices
National law and practice vary from country to country. A country may be based on the common law system, such as England, the civil law system, such as France, or on Islamic (Sharia) law, as in Saudi Arabia. Different issues and problems will arise according to the cultural, legislative and judicial context.

The local UNHCR legal adviser or protection officer must be familiar with the national criminal and civil law on the subject of rape and sexual violence in general. Research should include a review of the relevant legal provisions, rules of criminal procedure, role of the authorities and any medical requirements. The advice of legal counsel familiar with the domestic law and procedure should be sought.

Research should take place before an incident occurs in order to know, in advance, what procedural steps should be taken in the particular country and what advice should be given to refugee victims of sexual violence.

In addition to being familiar with the law and prepared to assist a refugee victim of sexual violence, it may be appropriate in some countries for a UNHCR or NGO staff member to accompany the victim in any dealings with the police. UNHCR should adopt a supportive role once a local lawyer has been appointed, but care must be taken to ensure that the legal counsel diligently represents the victim.

Examples of Relevant Information to be Researched
Defining the Applicable Legal Standards

- What is the applicable law and procedure?
- What is the legal definition of rape?
- What are the legal definitions of other forms of sexual violence?
- Does the offense of "statutory rape" exist?

Instigating Legal Proceedings
Reporting

- What are the legal requirements for reporting an incident of sexual violence?
- Is there, for example, a time limit for reporting an incident?

Legal Proceedings
- What type of legal procedure is applicable and/or appropriate?
- In criminal proceedings, is it the responsibility of the victim to press charges or is this at the discretion of the State?
- Is the option of commencing civil proceedings open to the victim, in addition or as an alternative, to criminal action?
- What are the evidentiary requirements?
- Is witness corroboration necessary?
- What is the requisite standard of proof?
- What is the likely time frame?
- Are there any special medical forms to be completed by the examining doctor in relation lo possible court proceedings?
- Are there any special procedures relating to child victims of sexual abuse?
- Are there any special programmes operating, such as the victim/advocate system?
- Are there any other legal provisions that are relevant to protection, assistance and counselling?

Protection of Victims and Witnesses
- Are there any specific legal provisions that are relevant to protection of the victim and witnesses giving testimony?

Traditions and customs of the refugee community

Some refugee communities may have traditional means of responding to incidents of sexual violence within their community.

- What are these traditional procedures?
- Are they fair, just and in accordance with international human r i g h t s standards?
- In particular, do they take into account the interests and protection requirements of the victim?
- Do they take into account the protection of the refugee community?

Sentences or Punishment
- If conviction is obtained, what is the likely sentence or punishment to be given to the perpetrator?

Compensation
- Are there any procedures through which a victim can apply for compensation?

Costs
- Is the burden on the State or on the individual?
- What are the likely financial costs to the victim of any legal proceedings?
- Can a victim obtain any legal aid funding in the country of asylum?

Abortion
- What are the laws in relation to abortion?
- If abortion is generally illegal, are there any special circumstances under which it may be allowed? (For example, where a woman becomes pregnant as a result of rape, where the life of the baby or the woman is endangered, or where there are reasons in relation to the psychological welfare of the woman).
- What evidence is needed to satisfy the special circumstances, e.g. medical reports?

4.2 International Law

International law prohibits sexual violence. This prohibition is found in several international human rights instruments as well as in customary international law.

Even if international law may not be applied at a national level, it may be useful in discussions with the authorities in reinforcing a point. It is therefore essential to be aware of the international norms which may be violated when sexual violence occurs.

Stress[es] the importance of international instruments relating to refugees, human rights and humanitarian law for the protection of asylum-seekers, refugees and returnees against sexual violence,

Executive Committee Conclusion No. 73 (XLIV) (1993), Preamble
Refugee Protection and Sexual Violence

a) The Declaration on the Elimination of Violence against Women (1993)
- This is the first set of international standards dealing specifically with violence against women.
- The Declaration was adopted, without a vote, by the General Assembly at its forty-eighth session in 1993. (Resolution 48/104 of 20 December 1993).
- It affirms that violence against women constitutes a violation of the rights and fundamental freedoms of women and impairs or nullifies their enjoyment of those rights and freedoms.
- It recognizes that effective implementation of the Convention on the Elimination of All Forms of Discrimination against Women would contribute to the elimination of violence against women.
- It is noted in the preamble that refugee women are "especially vulnerable to violence.

The Declaration is reproduced in Annex 6.

b) Systematic Mass Rape as a Crime against Humanity
- A report in 1993 by the Secretary-General of the United Nations to the Security Council specifically includes within the definition of "crimes against humanity" any acts of rape which are committed "as part of a widespread or systematic attack against any civilian population on national, political, ethnic, racial or religious grounds". It is noteworthy that systematic mass rape is an offence covered by the International Criminal Tribunal for Former Yugoslavia and the International Criminal Tribunal for Rwanda.

c) Appointment of a Special Rapporteur on violence against women

- In 1994 the Commission on Human Rights appointed a Special Rapporteur on violence against women for a three-year period. (Resolution 1994/45 entitled "The question of integrating the rights of women into the human rights mechanism of the United Nations and the elimination of violence against women"). The Special Rapporteur's preliminary report outlines the most basic issues with regard to violence against refugee and internally displaced women and makes preliminary recommendations, which in the most part have been incorporated in these Guidelines.

Providing information

- The Special Rapporteur is mandated, inter alia, to seek and receive information on any forms of violence against women. In this connection, UNHCR and NGOs can contribute significantly to the work of the Special Rapporteur by forwarding information on violence against women and by providing accurate, current data and statistics. A standard format for documenting violations of human rights of women is being developed by the Special Rapporteur and may be obtained from the Centre for Human Rights in Geneva. (Palais des Nations, 8-14 avenue de la Paix, 1211 Geneva 10, Switzerland. Fax: (41 22) 917 0212).

Promoting Awareness

- Readers of these Guidelines are encouraged to inform national and regional non-governmental organizations active in the field of women's human rights of the appointment of the Special Rapporteur to enable the establishment of a wide network for the collection and dissemination of information on this issue.

National Plans of Action

- The Special Rapporteur is calling upon all Governments to elaborate and implement a national plan of action on violence against women, as suggested in the Declaration on the Elimination of Violence against Women. UNHCR field staff should enquire about the existence of such a plan of action with the relevant authorities and ensure the inclusion of a component on violence against refugee women. UNHCR and other field staff, in cooperation with the Governments concerned, may be instrumental in the implementation of national plans of action, which, inter alia, call for the provision of specialized assistance for the support and rehabilitation of women victims of violence and for the initiation of strategies to develop legal and administrative mechanisms to ensure effective justice for these women.

d) Treaty monitoring bodies

Some of the human rights conventions have created treaty bodies to monitor the implementation and compliance of the conventions.

Examples are:

- The Committee on the Rights of the Child established under the Convention on the Rights of the Child (Article 43)
- The Committee on the Elimination of Discrimination against Women (CEDAW) established under the Convention on the Elimination of All Forms of Discrimination Against Women (Article 17)
- The Committee against Torture established under the Convention against Torture (Article 17)
- The Human Rights Committee established under the International Covenant on Civil and Political Rights (Article 28)
- The Committee on Economic, Social and Cultural Rights established by ECOSOC Resolution 1985/17

States are required to submit reports on a periodic basis to these Committees. Specifically in relation to the Committee on the Elimination of Discrimination against Women (CEDAW), in 1989 the Committee requested that States include in their reports information about violence against women and the measures taken to eliminate such violence. (General Recommendation No. 12).

e) Suggested action which UNHCR Staff and NGOs can take in the field

Awareness

- Find out what international instruments have been ratified by the State and how these have been incorporated into national law.
- Find out what international instruments have not been ratified and ascertain the reasons for not doing so. Similarly, find out whether the State has made any reservations to international instruments, and if so the reasons for these.

Lobbying

- Lobby for the ratification of instruments and withdrawal of any reservations.

Promotion

- Promote and disseminate international norms to raise awareness.

- Draw attention, as appropriate, to the nature, severity and magnitude of the problem of sexual violence against refugees.

Influence Reporting of States to Treaty Bodies
- Be involved in the preparation of country reports to the various treaty bodies by finding out which government section is writing them and provide input on any concerns.
- Lobby for fair and thorough reporting by States to the treaty bodies.

Provide Information to UNHCR Headquarters
- Reporting to UNHCR Headquarters on violations by a State of its international obligations relating to refugees will enable UNHCR to raise these concerns with the appropriate treaty bodies who can raise these issues with the State concerned.

Monitoring
- Be active in monitoring any recommendations made to the State by the treaty bodies. Such recommendations could include that the State amend its national legislation, the State improve practices, or that the State undertake special protection or assistance programmes and activities on behalf of refugees.

Training
- Include in training sessions of government officials, such as police, military and immigration officers, information on the various international obligations as undertaken by the State and their incorporation into national laws.

In Situations of Armed Conflict
- Join the International Committee of the Red Cross (ICRC), and others, in disseminating international humanitarian law and lobbying the parties to the conflict to respect these principles.

Refer to the UNHCR Training Module Human Rights and Refugee Protection, 1995, for more detailed discussion.

f) The International Instruments Relevant to Sexual Violence include the following:

The Universal Declaration of Human Rights (1948)
Article 3 Everyone has the right to life, liberty and security of person.
Article 5 No one shall be subjected to torture or to cruel, inhuman or degrading treatment or punishment.

The International Covenant on Civil and Political Rights (1966)
Article 7   No one shall be subjected to torture or to cruel, inhuman or degrading treatment or punishment
Article 91 Everyone has the right to liberty and security of person...
Article 101   All persons deprived of their liberty shall be treated with humanity and with respect for the inherent dignity of the human person.

The International Covenant on Economic, Social and Cultural Rights (1966)
Article 12 The States Parties to the present Covenant recognize the right of everyone to the enjoyment of the highest attainable standard of physical and mental health.

The Convention on the Elimination of All Forms of Discrimination against Women (1979)
Article 6 States Parties shall take all appropriate measures, including legislation, to suppress all forms of traffic in women and exploitation of prostitution of women.

In 1992 the Committee on the Elimination of Discrimination against Women (CEDAW) issued a recommendation (General recommendation No. 19) dealing exclusively with violence against women. The Committee stated that gender-based violence is a form of discrimination which seriously inhibits a woman's ability to enjoy rights and freedoms on an equal basis with men. They defined gender-based violence as that which is directed against a woman because she is a woman or which affects women disproportionately. They included "sexual harm or suffering" and "threats of such acts" as constituting gender-based violence. They noted that: "Gender-based violence may breach specific provisions of the Convention, regardless whether those provisions expressly mention violence".

The UN Convention against Torture and Other Cruel, Inhuman or Degrading Treatment or Punishment (1984)

Article 16 requires, inter alia, that the State "prevent... acts of cruel, inhuman or degrading treatment or punishment..., when such acts are committed by or at the instigation of or with the consent or acquiescence of a public official or other person acting in an official capacity...."

The Convention on the Rights of the Child (1989)
Article 19 Protection from Abuse and Neglect
1. States Parties shall take all appropriate legislative, administrative, social and educational measures to protect the child from all forms of physical or mental violence, injury or abuse, neglect or negligent treatment, maltreatment or exploitation, including sexual abuse, while in the care of parent(s), legal guardian(s) or any other person who has the care of the child.
2. Such protective measures should, as appropriate, include effective procedures for the establishment of social programmes to provide necessary support for the child and for those who have the care of the child, as well as for other forms of prevention and for identification, reporting, referral, investigation, treatment and follow-up of instances of child maltreatment described heretofore, and, as appropriate, for judicial involvement.
Article 24 Health and Health Services
3. States Parties shall take all effective and appropriate measures with a view to abolishing traditional practices prejudicial to the health of children.
Article 34 Sexual Exploitation
States Parties undertake to protect the child from all forms of sexual exploitation and sexual abuse. For these purposes, States Parties shall in particular take all appropriate national, bilateral and multilateral measures to prevent;
  (a) The inducement or coercion of a child to engage in any unlawful sexual activity.
  (b) The exploitative use of children in prostitution or other unlawful sexual practices.
  (c) The exploitative use of children in pornographic performances and materials.
Article 37 Torture and Deprivation of Liberty
  (a) No child shall be subjected to torture or other cruel, inhuman or degrading treatment or punishment
  (b) Every child deprived of liberty shall be treated with humanity and respect of the inherent dignity of the human person
Article 39 Rehabilitative Care
States Parties shall take all appropriate measures to promote physical and psychological recovery and social reintegration of a child victim of: any form of

neglect, exploitation, or abuse; torture or any other form of cruel, inhuman or degrading treatment or punishment; or armed conflicts. Such recovery and reintegration shall take place in an environment which fosters the health, self-respect and dignity of the child.

REGIONAL INSTRUMENTS

• Europe
The European Convention for the Protection of Human Rights and Fundamental Freedoms (1950)
Article 3 No one shall be subjected to torture or to inhuman or degrading treatment or punishment.
Article 51. Every one has the right to liberty and security of person

• Americas
The American Convention on Human Rights (1969) ("Pact of San JosΘ, Costa Rica")
Article 5 Right to Humane Treatment
1. Every person has the right to have his physical, mental, and moral integrity respected.
2. No one shall be subjected to torture or to cruel, inhuman, or degrading punishment or treatment. All persons deprived of their liberty shall be treated with respect for the inherent dignity of the human person.
Article 7 Right to Personal Liberty
1. Every person has the right to personal liberty and security.

The Inter-American Convention on the Prevention, Punishment and Eradication of Violence against Women (Convention of BelΘm do Para) (1994)
Article 7 sets out State obligations in regard to the eradication of gender-based violence.
Article 8 sets out additional obligations regarding education and the development of a mass consciousness in relation to violence against women.
Article 10 obliges the States parties to include in their national reports to the Inter-American Commission of Women information on measures adopted to prevent and prohibit violence against women and to assist women affected by violence, as well as any difficulties they observe in applying those measures, and the factors that contribute to violence against women.

Article 12 provides for an individual right of petition and a right for non-governmental organizations to lodge complaints with the Inter-American Commission of Human Rights.

- **Africa**

The African Charter on Human and Peoples' Rights (1981)

Article 4 Human beings are inviolable. Every human being shall be entitled to respect for this life and the integrity of his person. No one may be arbitrarily deprived of this right.

Article 5 Every individual shall have the right to the respect of the dignity inherent in a human being and to the recognition of his legal status. All forms of exploitation and degradation of man particularly slavery, slave trade, torture, cruel, inhuman or degrading punishment and treatment shall be prohibited.

Article 6 Every individual shall have the right to liberty and the security of his person

INTERNATIONAL HUMANITARIAN LAW

International Humanitarian Law is the body of law which governs situations of armed conflict, whether they be of an international or non-international character. Persons of concern to UNHCR, most particularly returnees and internally displaced persons, may be found in situations of armed conflict governed by international humanitarian law.

- **International Armed Conflicts**

The Geneva Convention Relative to the Protection of Civilian Persons in Time of War (The Fourth Geneva Convention) (1949)

Article 27 [Protected persons]... shall at all times be humanely treated, and shall be protected especially against all acts of violence or threats thereof and against insults and public curiosity. Women shall be especially protected against any attack on their honour, in particular against rape, enforced prostitution, or any form of indecent assault.

Protocol I relating to the Protection of Victims of International Armed Conflicts (1977)

Article 51.2 The civilian population as such, as well as individual civilians, shall not be the object of attack. Acts or threats of violence the primary purpose of which is to spread terror among the civilian population are prohibited.

Article 75.2 Fundamental Guarantees

The following acts are and shall remain prohibited at any time and in any place whatsoever, whether committed by civilian or by military agents:

(a) violence to the life, health, or physical or mental well-being of persons, in particular

(i) murder,

(ii) torture of all kinds, whether physical or mental,

(iii) corporal punishment; and

(iv) mutilation;

(b) outrages upon personal dignity, in particular humiliating and degrading treatment, enforced prostitution and any form of indecent assault;

...

(e) threats to commit any of the foregoing acts.

Article 76 Protection of women

1. Women shall be the subject of special respect and shall be protected in particular against rape, forced prostitution and any other form of indecent assault.

Article 77 Protection of children

1. Children shall be the object of special respect and shall be protected against any form of indecent assault.

- **Non-International Armed Conflicts**

The Geneva Conventions (1949)

Article 3 the following acts are and shall remain prohibited at any time and in any place whatsoever with respect to [persons taking no active part in the hostilities...]:

(a) violence to life and person, in particular... mutilation, cruel treatment and torture;

(c) outrages upon personal dignity, in particular, humiliating and degrading treatment;...

Protocol II relating to the Protection of Victims of Non-International Armed Conflicts (1977)

Article 4 Fundamental guarantees

2....the following acts against [all persons who do not take a direct part in or who have ceased to take part in hostilities] are and shall remain prohibited at any time and in any place whatsoever.

(a) violence to the life, health and physical or mental well-being of persons, in particular murder as well as cruel treatment such as torture, mutilation or any form of corporal punishment;

(e) outrages upon personal dignity, in particular humiliating and degrading treatment, rape, enforced prostitution and any form of indecent assault;
(h) threats to commit any of the foregoing acts.

Also see the Declaration on the Protection of Women and Children in Emergency and Armed Conflict, General Assembly resolution 3318 (XXIX) of 14 December 1974.

The Declaration on the Elimination of Violence against Women (See 4.2(a) above and Annex 6).

4.3 Refugee Status Determination

Strongly condemns persecution through sexual violence, which not only constitutes a gross violation of human rights, as well as, when committed in the context of armed conflict, a grave breach of humanitarian law, but is also a particularly serious offense to human dignity;

Executive Conclusion No. 73 (XLIV) (1993), paragraph (a)
Refugee Protection and Sexual Violence

Calls upon States and UNHCR to ensure the equal access of women and men to refugee status determination...

Executive Committee Conclusion No. 73 (XLIV) (1993), paragraph (c)
Refugee Protection and Sexual Violence

Acts of sexual violence may bear on the refugee status determination process both for the applicant who is a victim and for the applicant or refugee status holder who is a perpetrator.

a) The Victim
Victims of sexual violence might not be forthcoming with this information at the outset and this reluctance to report sexual violence may have significant effects on refugee status determination. Experience has clearly shown that incidents may not come to light until refugees have been resettled and seek therapy which may be months or even years later. Individuals may have contact with many refugee workers without sometimes ever disclosing their experience. Information disclosed later by the victim may be disregarded, and may even be considered to reflect

negatively on the credibility of the applicant. Paragraphs 57 through 61 of UNHCR's Guidelines on the Protection of Refugee Women provide guidance.

Recommends that in procedures for the determination of refugee status, asylum-seekers who may have suffered sexual violence be treated with particular sensitivity;

Executive Committee Conclusion No. 73 (XLIV) (1993), paragraph (g) Refugee Protection and Sexual Violence

Recommends the development by States of appropriate guidelines on women asylum-seekers, in recognition of the fact that women refugees often experience persecution differently from refugee men;

Executive Committee Conclusion No. 73 (XLIV) (1993), paragraph (e) Refugee Protection and Sexual Violence

In this context, it is essential that status determination officers be conscious of possible reactions to trauma (see, for instance 3.9 a) Common Psychological Reactions) and are familiar with culturally different patterns of behaviour and language. The statement by the asylum applicant to have been "badly treated" may be an euphemism for rape. Training of the relevant officials is therefore highly recommended.

Recommends the establishment by States of training programmes designed to ensure that those involved in the refugee status determination process are adequately sensitized to issues of gender and culture;

Executive Committee Conclusion No. 73 (XLIV) (1993), paragraph (j) Refugee Protection and Sexual Violence

When rape or other forms of sexual violence are committed for reasons of race, religion, nationality, membership of a particular social group or political opinion, it may be considered persecution under the definition of the term "refugee" in the Statute of the Office (paragraph 6.A(ii)) and the 1951 Convention relating to the Status of Refugees (Article 1A(2)) if it is perpetrated or "knowingly tolerated by the authorities, or if the authorities refuse, or prove unable, to offer effective protection". (UNHCR *Handbook on Procedures and Criteria for Determining Refugee Status* (1992), paragraph 65)).

Supports the recognition as refugees of persons whose claim to refugee status is based upon a well-founded fear of persecution, through sexual violence, for reasons of race, religion, nationality, membership of a particular social group or political opinion,

Executive Committee Conclusion No. 73 (XLIV) (1993), paragraph (d)
Refugee Protection and Sexual Violence

Recognize[s] that States, in the exercise of their sovereignty, are free to adopt the interpretation that women asylum-seekers who face harsh or inhuman treatment due to having transgressed the social mores of the society in which they live may be considered as a "particular social group" within the meaning of Article 1 A(2) of the 1951 United Nations Refugee Convention,

Executive Committee Conclusion No. 39 (XXXVI) (1985), paragraph (k)
Refugee Women and International Protection

A well-founded fear of sexual violence in such circumstances can thus provide the basis for a claim to refugee status. The experience of rape or sexual torture as a form of persecution might also constitute "compelling reasons arising out of previous persecution" for not applying the cessation clauses in Article 1 C (S) and (6) of the 1951 Convention.

In certain societies, a rape victim may be killed or banished, or considered to have no alternative but to marry her attacker or become a prostitute û all additional human rights violations. Where the return to the country of origin would have one of these results, and where no other basis for her recognition has been identified, she may be considered a refugee sur place.

b) The Perpetrator

A particular situation may arise where the alleged perpetrator of an act of sexual violence is a recognized refugee or an asylum-seeker whose claim to refugee status has not yet been finally determined.

The mere suspicion or an accusation against such a person should have no immediate consequences as far as that person's status is concerned, nor should it affect the continuation of the eligibility procedure. However, as a refugee or asylum-seeker, he is subject to the laws of the country of asylum and may therefore be subject to detention during the investigation of the crime or pending trial.

Should he be convicted by a final judgment of the judiciary in the country of asylum of having committed sexual violence, it is only in the most extreme circumstances that such conviction, apart from the penal sanction, also should affect his status as a refugee or asylum-seeker in the country.

The relevant provisions of the 1951 Convention dealing with the question of refugees who have committed crimes are found in Article 1 F on Exclusion, Article 32 on Expulsion, and Article 33 on Non-Refoulement. Both Article 32 and Article 33 require, as a precondition for any measures involving the expulsion or refoulement of the refugee, that the crime(s) he has been convicted of are of such grave character, that the refugee constitutes a "threat to the national security or public order (of the country of asylum)" (Article 32) or "a danger to the community of that country" (Article 33).

Acts of sexual violence, while grave, are seldom in themselves sufficient basis for expelling or refouling a refugee, except, perhaps, in situations of repeated offenses after a first conviction. The same applies for asylum-seekers, as they may be refugees and therefore fall under the 1951 Convention. The status of asylum seekers convicted for acts of sexual violence should therefore be determined prior to making any decision regarding expulsion.

Article 1 F deals with the question of the exclusion of persons from refugee status on the grounds that they do not deserve international protection. For a more detailed elaboration on the applicability of the exclusion clauses, please refer to the UNHCR Handbook on Procedures and Criteria for Determining Refugee Status, paragraphs 147-163.

A central point in applying the exclusion clauses, as noted in paragraph 156 of the Handbook, is the need to strike a balance between the nature of the offence allegedly committed by the asylum-seeker and the degree of persecution feared. If a person has a well-founded fear of very severe persecution, e.g. persecution endangering his life or freedom, a crime must be very grave in order to exclude him.